BEHIND THE CAMERA

James Cameron

Ron Howard

Spike Lee

George Lucas

Rob Reiner

Steven Spielberg

James Cameron

Bonnie McMeans

Chelsea House Publishers
Philadelphia

Frontis piece: Cameron accepts the Oscar for Best Director for his 1997 film *Titanic*. Quoting a memorable line from the film, Cameron raised his arms and declared, "I'm king of the world!"

CHELSEA HOUSE PUBLISHERS

EDITOR IN CHIEF Sally Cheney
DIRECTOR OF PRODUCTION Kim Shinners
CREATIVE MANAGER Takeshi Takahashi
MANUFACTURING MANAGER Diann Grasse

STAFF FOR JAMES CAMERON

ASSOCIATE EDITOR Ben Kim
PRODUCTION ASSISTANT Jaimie Winkler
PICTURE RESEARCHER Sarah Bloom
SERIES AND COVER DESIGNER Takeshi Takahashi
LAYOUT 21st Century Publishing and Communications, Inc.

http://www.chelseahouse.com

First Printing

1 3 5 7 9 8 6 4 2

Library of Congress Cataloging-in-Publication Data

CIP appied for ISBN 0-7910-6713-0

Table of Contents

James Cameron and his wife, actress Linda Hamilton, wave to the crowd after their arrival at the 1998 Golden Globe Awards. Cameron was presented with the Best Director award for his film *Titanic*.

Chapter 1

"King of the World"

MARCH 23, 1998, James Cameron hit Hollywood's equivalent of a grand slam in the Shrine Auditorium in Los Angeles, California. During the 70th Annual Academy Awards, Cameron's *Titanic,* released December 19 and starring Kate Winslet and Leonardo DiCaprio, won 11 Oscars, the second film in movie history to do so. It was a fitting tribute to the Canadian writer, director, and producer responsible for box office hits like *The Terminator, Aliens, Terminator 2: Judgment Day*, and *True Lies*.

Cameron's achievement was not without personal and

financial sacrifice. Despite the real Titanic going down on her maiden voyage April 15, 1912, after hitting an iceberg, Cameron had spent several years trying to keep his *Titanic* afloat.

He talked his way onto two Russian submarines the size of minivans to film the wreck of the *Titanic* 12,480 feet beneath the North Atlantic Ocean. He helped invent a crush-proof casing for a remote-controlled camera that could move around *inside* the ship instead of filming through the portholes. He convinced Twentieth Century Fox to build a 17-million gallon tank in Baja, Mexico, to hold a 775-foot recreation of the great ship, which he would eventually have to *sink*.

Budgeting and scheduling problems plagued the film-maker from the start. When Fox threatened to sink Cameron's *Titanic* prematurely, Cameron volunteered to give up his salary and percentage of the film's profits as compensation for going $100 million over budget and lagging several months behind schedule. (Studio executives had hoped for a summer blockbuster.) Cameron preferred to sacrifice his profits rather than "work for three years . . . and make a bad movie."

Now Cameron's determination to prove naysayers wrong was paying off. The concept he had pitched to Fox studios—"Think of Romeo and Juliet on a boat"—had materialized into a film which had earned $350 million after just 58 days in theaters. Not even Steven Spielberg's *Jurassic Park* had been so successful, breaking only $300 million after 67 days.

Later, Cameron would tell reporters he was "a little mystified" by public reaction to *Titanic*. He knew the film was good, but neither he nor Fox Studios and Paramount Pictures had expected a 20 percent repeat audience (instead of the usual two percent). In other words, people were seeing the movie three and four times.

The movie had achieved unbelievable international acclaim as well, earning $89 million in just four weeks. In France, Germany, and Spain, *Titanic* ticket sales accounted for 50 percent of box office profits. Jorge Carreon, a spokesperson for 20th Century Fox International, reported that in Paris, "lineups were so huge, police had to be called in to several theaters for crowd control." *Newsweek* magazine reported that ticket sales elsewhere in France exceeded local populations. And everywhere Cameron visited to promote his film, whether it was Moscow, Tokyo, or Rome, he noticed audiences "all cried in the same places [in the movie]."

Cameron's novelization of the screenplay was on the *New York Times* bestseller list, and the *Titanic* soundtrack was number one on the charts for 10 consecutive weeks.

Accolades were pouring in. January 18, the Hollywood Foreign Press Association presented Cameron with two Golden Globe Awards for Best Director and Best Picture. In his acceptance speech, Cameron jokingly alluded to the problems that had plagued the *Titanic* project from the start: "I just think we should give a big round of applause for the people who had the *huevos* to make this movie. What the hell were they thinking?"

Six weeks later, Cameron received the 50th Annual Directors Guild of America Feature Film Award, a sure indication he was now a serious contender for a Best Director Oscar at the upcoming Academy Awards only 16 days away. Accepting the Directors Guild Award, the self-described "techno-nerd" remarked: "I used to always say I made movies and not films. *Remains of the Day* is a film. *Terminator 2* is a movie. Now that I have this, I may

James Cameron with Gloria Stuart, shown here receiving her own star on the Hollywood Walk of Fame on September 27, 2000.

have to admit that I may have inadvertently made a film."

Best of all, the Academy of Motion Picture Arts and Sciences had announced 14 nominations, including Best Picture and Best Director. In fact, *Titanic* was tied with *All About Eve* (1950) for the most nominations ever received.

Although Cameron was excited about going to the 1998 Academy Awards, this was not the first time one of his films had been nominated for or won an Oscar. Prior to *Titanic's* success, Cameron had earned a reputation for writing compelling screenplays and directing action-packed thrillers in the science fiction genre. He had also earned a reputation for being a "perfectionist" and a "screaming tyrant" on the set.

Cameron's first movie to receive an Academy Award nomination was *Aliens* (1986). In the film, a space mining engineer (Sigourney Weaver) leads marines against a colony of extraterrestrial creatures which hatch their young in human stomachs. The film earned seven Academy Award nominations, including Best Actress for Sigourney Weaver, and won Oscars for Visual Effects and Sound Effects Editing.

The Abyss (1989), featuring deep-sea oil riggers and Navy SEALs who encounter benign, watery beings at the bottom of the Atlantic Ocean, received four Oscar nominations, winning for Visual Effects again. Like-wise, *Terminator 2: Judgment Day* (1991), in which Arnold Schwarzenegger's character returns to the screen to rescue a young John Connor and his mother from another futuristic hit man, won Oscars in four of the six categories for which it had received nominations: Sound, Sound Effects Editing, Visual Effects, and Makeup.

Even though these films did not win Cameron any nominations for Best Director or Best Picture, he took satisfaction in knowing that he had written and directed enormously popular movies and had started his own production company, Lightstorm Entertainment (1990), and special effects company, Digital Domain (1993).

Now it was Oscar night again, and no one could stop talking about the movie that had proven to be unsinkable. *Titanic* had cost about $200 million to make, but had made over $1.2 billion so far. It was the most expensive and most profitable film in movie history.

In addition to Academy Award nominations for Best Picture and Best Director, there were also nominations for Best Actress, Best Supporting Actress, Best Cinematography, Best Costume Design, Best Editing, Best Makeup, Best Art Direction, Best Score, Best Song, Best Sound, Best Sound Effects Editing, and Best Visual Effects.

Cameron and his fourth wife, Linda Hamilton, star of *Terminator* and *Terminator 2*, walked down the red carpet into Shrine Auditorium amidst throngs of movie fans, celebrities, well-wishers, and reporters snapping pictures and seeking comments. Hamilton was beaming with pride and called Cameron her "hero," adding, "He's the hardest working man I have ever seen." Cameron declared he was "very happy—happy to be part of this madness."

Inside the auditorium, host Billy Crystal opened with a good-natured jab at Cameron's film: "Here we are on the *Titanic*—big, expensive, and everyone wants it to go faster."

As usual, the Best Supporting Actress award is announced first, and this went to Kim Basinger for *L.A. Confidential*. *Titanic* fans were a little disappointed. They had hoped Gloria Stuart, the actress who played the

In a scene from *Titanic*, Bill Paxton, Gloria Stuart, and Suzy Amis view artifacts from the wreck. Cameron had hoped Gloria Stewart would win the Oscar for Best Supporting Actress for her role as the older Rose DeWitt Bukater.

older version of Kate Winslet's character, Rose DeWitt Bukater, would win. Then Titanic might have had a better chance to break the record for the most Oscars, set by *Ben-Hur* in 1959. *Ben-Hur* won 11 Oscars and no movie since then has won more.

When the second Oscar, for Best Costume Design, went to *Titanic,* the excitement in the auditorium intensified. Perhaps *Titanic* had a chance to break the record after all. Costume Designer Deborah Scott graciously accepted the prize and thanked James Cameron for the "first class passage."

Next came Robin Williams, who won Best Supporting Actor for his role in *Good Will Hunting.* Then *Titanic* took center stage again for the next three Oscars awarded for Best Sound, Best Sound Effects Editing, and Best Visual Effects.

The Best Dramatic Score Award went to *Titanic's* James Horner, who expressed appreciation for being able to work on such a "history-making project."

At last, James Cameron's name was called for the Award for Best Editing. Although Cameron shared the award with Conrad Buff, all eyes were on Cameron as he raised his Oscar high and addressed his young daughter Josephine at home watching the event on television: "This is the thing I described to you, the Oscar. It is a really cool thing to get."

Celine Dion sang her hit record and *Titanic's* theme song, "My Heart Will Go On" to thunderous applause, after which James Horner received his second Oscar for Best Song. Before he left the stage, he thanked Cameron "for being in a good mood the day I brought you this song."

Following Ben Affleck and Matt Damon's presentation of Oscars in the Long and Short Documentary categories, *Titanic*'s art department won the Art Direction Award for their brilliant and authentic depiction of the ship right down to the silverware.

Shortly thereafter, Affleck and Damon won the Best Original Screenplay Oscar for *Good Will Hunting.* Cameron's screenplay had not been nominated and, in fact, had been ridiculed by some movie critics as being mediocre.

Jack Nicholson won Best Actor for *As Good As It Gets* and joked, "I've had a sinking feeling all night . . . ." Likewise, Helen Hunt won Best Actress for her role opposite Nicholson, to the disappointment of Kate Winslet fans, for Winslet had also been nominated for Best Actress.

Surprisingly, the Best Cinematography Award went to *Titanic,* defeating Martin Scorsese's critically acclaimed *Kundun.* Russell Carpenter accepted the award, saying: "What a year it's been. It [*Titanic*] has gone from a ship of fools to being a ship of dreams."

Now with the end of the evening drawing closer, only two Oscars remained: Best Director and Best Picture. The Shrine Auditorium was quiet with nervous anticipation. Warren Beatty opened up the envelope and announced: " . . . and the Oscar for Best Director goes to . . . James Cameron for *Titanic!"*

Immediately, James Cameron hugged his wife, acknowledged Arnold Schwarzenegger sitting nearby, and leaped up onto the stage. Proudly holding his Oscar, he addressed the audience: "I don't know about you, but I am having a really good time."

He went on to thank his brother Mike, who worked for Lightstorm Entertainment, and his assistant director Josh McLaglen. Next came warm words for his wife, children, and parents. Then to everyone's delight, Cameron mimicked *Titanic's* Jack Dawson (DiCaprio) by thrusting his arms in the air and yelling, "I'm king of the world!"

Typically, when a director receives an Oscar for Best Director, he also receives the Oscar for Best Picture. So it came as no surprise when Sean Connery announced *Titanic* as the winner of Best Picture. A jubilant James

In *Titanic*, Leonardo DiCaprio and Danny Nucci play two young impoverished travelers who win their tickets to America in a card game. Here, DiCaprio's character, artist Jack Dawson, stands at the prow of the ship and declares himself "king of the world."

Cameron took the stage for the third time along with co-producer Jon Landau.

After Landau made his acceptance speech, Cameron began by saying, "We are here to celebrate the magic of motion pictures, and I feel privileged to be a part of that magic." Then Cameron asked for a moment of silence in memory of the "1,500 men, women, and children who died."

Somberly, he also asked the audience to listen to the beatings of their own hearts, "the most important thing of all." He concluded with, "Okay, now let's go party till dawn."

Cameron had something else to celebrate. In lieu of the film's "gargantuan success," arrangements were underway for the studios to pay Cameron an estimated $100 million for his services, thereby dissolving Cameron's verbal offer to forego payment, an offer that was never legally finalized and documented anyway, according to Cameron.

Truly, the "techno-nerd" from Niagara Falls, Canada, had become "King of the World."

James Cameron grew up in Chippewa, Ontario, a suburb just north of Niagara Falls. After getting bitten by the filmmaking bug, he knew that he would have to move out of Chippewa in order to pursue his dream of making movies.

Chapter 2

From Chippewa to Hollywood

IN THE LATE sixties, while America coped with Vietnam War protesters burning draft cards and chanting "Make love, not war," Jim Cameron, a high school student at Stamford Collegiate in Chippewa, Ontario, was reading Spiderman comic books carefully hidden inside his textbooks.

When he wasn't reading about his favorite action hero, he was building model spaceships, writing plays and stories, or drawing pictures of Etruscan helmets and dinosaur bones at the Royal Ontario Museum in Toronto.

Most of all, he was daydreaming . . . about making movies.

James Cameron was born on August 16, 1954, the eldest of five. His family lived in Kapuskasing, a town of about 9,000 people in northwestern Ontario and the site of a World War I prisoner of war camp. Jim's father, Philip, was an electrical engineer for the Spruce Falls Paper and Saw Mill built in 1922 to tap the energy of a powerful waterfall called Smokey Falls.

His mother, Shirley, was a homemaker and a landscape artist. Philip Cameron had a reputation for being a strict disciplinarian, while Shirley nurtured Jim's artistic talents. A strong-willed and independent woman, Shirley Cameron once convinced a local gallery to show some of her young son's paintings.

When Jim was very young, the family moved to Chippewa, a suburb just north of Niagara Falls. Chippewa was originally a town named for the Chippewa Indians, who were forced to live on reservations in the United States and Canada during the 19th century.

Growing up in Chippewa, Jim and his younger brother Mike were considered nerds. Unlike other boys who spent their weekends playing sports or watching television, the Cameron boys were always building or inventing something, like a rock catapult so well-engineered that the rocks made craters in the ground upon impact.

According to Christopher Heard, author of Cameron's biography, *Dreaming Aloud,* Jim and his brother Mike were often targeted for being different. Heard describes one incident in which the Cameron boys decided to seek revenge against some bullies who had stolen some of their toys:

> Together they snuck into the offenders' yard and sawed through the branches that held their tree house in place. When the dirty little crooks next climbed into their tree house, the entire structure toppled to the ground, sending at least one of them to the hospital.

James was also reading, thanks to the encouragement of his paternal grandmother, Rose Cameron, who taught school. Completely devoted to his grandmother, Cameron would later name *Titanic's* heroine, Rose, after her, saying, "She instilled in me the love of literature." James also enjoyed reading science fiction authors Arthur C. Clarke, Ray Bradbury, and Robert Heinlein.

When James was not building, inventing, or reading, he was watching movies at the neighborhood theater. "As a child, I was fascinated by the imagination and creativity of film," he explains. "I remember seeing King Kong versus Godzilla and knowing I could create better special effects. I [later] developed a curiosity about camera shots and how cameras and zoom lenses worked."

Cameron's obsession with exploring how things worked was evident throughout his early teens in Chippewa; as a case in point, he and Mike once powered a kind of hot air balloon made out of dry cleaning bags and lit candles. This "UFO" was featured on the local news after the fire department was called to bring it down.

Another experiment involved putting a mouse in a home-made submersible to test the effects of pressurized breathing. Contrary to some reports, Cameron insists he never sent mice to their deaths in this homemade submersible over Niagara Falls. "I built a submersible out of a mayonnaise jar and an erector set and a paint bucket or something," he once told a reporter. "I put a mouse in it and lowered it down off the bridge to the bottom of Chippewa Creek and pulled it back up. The mouse was fine."

Although Cameron always enjoyed weekend matinees, his appreciation for good filmmaking intensified when he saw *2001: A Space Odyssey.* He was 15 years old and remembers vividly his reaction: "I just couldn't figure out

A pivotal moment for a 15-year-old James Cameron came when he saw the film *2001: A Space Odyssey*. Captivated by the movie's dramatic special effects, Cameron became determined to figure out how the film was made and to make movies of his own.

how all those visual effects were done, and I wanted badly to know, to understand what I was seeing. I went back to see the movie 10 times. . . . "

It was then Cameron knew he wanted to make movies. Borrowing his father's Super-8 camera, he began to build his own miniature spaceships and shoot "epic space battles" between them in his garage. At night, before falling asleep, he would choreograph film sequences in his mind, trying to figure out better ways to do them. Not having the technical knowledge or experience frustrated him, however, and he dreamed of moving to Hollywood where he could learn to create realistic special effects.

On the other hand, Cameron was a realist. He knew the likelihood of making movies in small-town Chippewa was pretty remote. "I had a fascination with it," he says, "but I couldn't see myself as a future film director. There was a definite feeling on my part that those people were somehow born into it, almost like a caste system. Little kids from a small town in Canada didn't get to direct movies."

Stuck in Chippewa, Cameron kept busy pursuing a variety of interests. He worked part-time in a pastry shop in what is now called Victoria Park Restaurant, overlooking Niagara Falls.

He entered and won local art contests like the 1968 Niagara District Art Association's Paint-Out. His brother Mike remembers that Cameron's pictures were always out of the ordinary. "He won all the Halloween window-painting contests," Mike says. "Everybody else would do some dumb pumpkin. He would do this wild, high-energy thing that had depth and proportion."

Cameron excelled at drawing. The 1971 Stamford Collegiate Yearbook features his illustration of the Stamford Monster, the school mascot. And many of Cameron's drawings and paintings still adorn the walls of his alma mater today.

He developed a love of history, inspired by his favorite high school teacher, Margaret Englund, who encouraged him to "dream and dream big." And dream he did. In fact, while daydreaming in 12th grade biology class, Cameron

Cameron's favorite comic book while growing up was *Spider-Man*, and he even went so far as to eventually write a screenplay for a movie treatment. He seemed to identify with Peter Parker's sense of alienation for his intellectual curiosity.

came up with the idea for *The Abyss,* which he would turn into a screenplay many years later.

Slowly, the young filmmaker was beginning to realize he had two passions: science and storytelling. "I had a narrative drive," Cameron says, "which I believe is psychologically inherent in some people. This drive goes all the way back to prehistoric times when people were sitting around a fire and someone was trying to make everyone laugh with his story about catching the biggest bison."

To satisfy his need to tell stories, Cameron started writing and producing plays for Stamford's theater arts department.

To satisfy his curiosity about how or why things worked, he joined the science club, eventually becoming president.

During this time, like director Steven Spielberg, Cameron seemed keenly aware that he was different and somewhat alienated from most young people his age. Paula Parisi, author of *Titanic and the Making of James Cameron*, refers to a "scriptment" Cameron later wrote for a feature film about his beloved action hero, Spiderman. Although Cameron's *Spiderman* was never made, Cameron's description of Peter Parker, the teenage scientist who becomes Spiderman, seems to reflect what Cameron himself may have been feeling as an adolescent:

> Peter is a bright kid. He doesn't have many friends. He is ostracized for his interest in science. Our MTV culture frowns on people who think too much. Intellectual curiosity is decidedly un-hip. Who cares about where the universe came from or how the Greeks hammered Troy? Did you hear the new Pearl Jam album?

Halfway through Cameron's senior year in high school, Philip Cameron made an important announcement. He was taking a new position in Orange County, California, and the family would move as soon as James graduated, possibly to Los Angeles. As soon as Cameron heard "Los Angeles," he asked his father, "Isn't that somewhere near Hollywood?" When his father said it was, Cameron could barely contain his excitement. Moving to Hollywood was exactly what Cameron had dreamed of doing. Perhaps now he would become the filmmaker he longed to be.

High school graduation did not come soon enough for Jim Cameron. As his family made plans to move to California, it probably never occurred to Cameron that he'd be invited back to Stamford Collegiate 24 years later for the dedication of the Cameron Theater in the school's brand new Barbara Frum Communications Center.

Once the Camerons settled in Orange County, Cameron realized that, without a driver's license, he was just as far away from Hollywood as when he lived in Canada. This depressed him a great deal. He also wanted to go directly to film school, but his parents couldn't afford the tuition, so he enrolled at California State University at Fullerton.

Initially, Cameron contemplated majoring in marine biology. After all, he had always loved and been fascinated by water, most likely because of his experiences growing up near major waterfalls. He was a certified scuba diver even though he had never been to the ocean. To Cameron, diving in lakes and rivers was like being in another world. And he enjoyed being transported to another world.

However, like many college students, Cameron really did not know what he should study in school. When he couldn't attend film school, he felt bewildered and uncertain as to how he could combine his two passions: science and story-telling. "I was pulled in a lot of different directions . . . " he recalls. "I didn't know if I wanted to be a scientist or an artist. I knew I had the temperament of an artist."

He decided to major in physics, then switched to English literature. Even though Cameron made good grades in his classes, obtaining a college degree suddenly seemed mean-ingless. So he dropped out of school and began to work odd jobs as a machinist, a truck driver, and a school bus driver.

By 1974, he was married to Sharon Williams, a waitress from a Bob's Big Boy restaurant he used to frequent. The first of five wives, Sharon would become the inspiration for the heroine, Sarah Connor, in *The Terminator* and *Terminator 2: Judgment Day*. The similarity between the two women is striking. Before Sarah Connor's world gets turned upside

When Cameron was a senior in high school, his father announced that his new job would involve moving the family to southern California—near Hollywood. Finally, it seemed like Cameron's dream of becoming a filmmaker was looking more and more like a reality—that is, until he realized that he needed a driver's license in order to travel around the Los Angeles area.

down by the Terminator, she is a waitress at Bob's Big Buns.

While married to Sharon Williams, Cameron drifted further and further away from his dream of becoming a filmmaker. Reflecting on that dark period in his life, he describes himself as someone who "liked to smoke dope and go to the river and drink beer and drive fast cars."

Then Cameron had a revelation.

In the summer of 1977, he went to see George Lucas' *Star Wars*. It changed his life. "I was really upset when I saw *Star Wars*," he said. "That was the movie I wanted to make. After seeing that movie, I got very determined. I decided to get busy."

Before seeing *Star Wars* in 1977, Cameron had begun to let his life drift away from his dream of being a filmmaker. But the big-budget sci-fi hit energized Cameron, spurring him on to study everything he could on scriptwriting, camera operation, and film direction.

Like a madman, Cameron began reading everything he could about filmmaking, boasting later that he gave himself a graduate school education for free, simply by visiting local libraries. He studied screenwriting and scrutinized scripts of his favorite movies. He devoured doctoral dissertations on camera operation and visual effects techniques. He bought bits and pieces of camera equipment to take apart and examine so he could figure out how they worked. He installed dolly tracks in his living room so he could freely move equipment about. He continued to write and paint at night.

Cameron also became friends with another aspiring

screenwriter and actor named William Wisher, who would later collaborate with Cameron on the screenplays for *The Terminator* and *Terminator 2: Judgment Day.* One year after the success of *Star Wars,* Cameron and Wisher decided to make a 10-minute science fiction film called *Xenogenesis.*

Together they wrote a screenplay about two humans, Laurie and Raj, who travel through space in search of a new Eden, a place where humans could begin the human race again.

Cameron and Wisher raised enough money to rent 35-mm camera equipment and a studio. They hired an actress, Margaret Undiel, to play Laurie, and Wisher played Raj. For special effects, Cameron and Wisher constructed their own models, sets, and matte paintings.

A matte painting simulates a background too difficult or expensive to create. Then live action or miniatures are filmed in front of the paintings. Matte paintings were originally painted on glass. Today many matte paintings are created on computer screens.

For James Cameron, it was his first chance to direct, and he has fond memories of the experience:

> It was a bit like a doctor doing his first appendectomy after having only read about it. We spent the first day of the shoot just trying to figure out how to get the camera running. Now I knew in theory how the threading path worked, but we couldn't get the camera to run to save our lives. There were three of us, and one of the guys was an engineer, so we simply took the camera apart, figured out how it worked, traced the circuitry, and then realized there was something in the camera that shut the camera off in case the film buckled.

Xenogenesis has since become a fascinating study of

Cameron's earliest days as a filmmaker. Movie fans enjoy pointing out similarities between *Xenogenesis* and Cameron's later films, particularly the *Terminator* movies, *Aliens,* and *The Abyss.*

The short film is a self-contained episode of a longer running series. At the beginning of the movie, white credits roll on a black background. Then a voice-over narration and series of paintings bring the audience up to date on past events leading up to this particular episode. One of the paintings shows a man with a mechanical arm, not unlike the scene in *Terminator* when Schwarzenegger pulls the flesh off his arm to expose his mechanical limb.

The first scene then depicts Raj exploring a huge, abandoned spaceship. Suddenly, he comes face to face with a menacing robot moving along a track, similar to the machines moving along identical tracks in *Terminator and Terminator 2*

As the robot attacks Raj, Laurie forces her way inside the spaceship, using a machine that she controls with joysticks, exactly the way Ripley does battle with the alien queen at the end of *Aliens.* Not only does the actress resemble Sigourney Weaver, but also the shots of her inside the machine are reminiscent of the shots of the actress, Mary Elizabeth Mastrantonio, in the miniature submarine in *The Abyss.*

A cliffhanger battle between Laurie and the robot ensues. Most importantly, like the strong, independent women Cameron favors in later films, it is Laurie who rescues Raj, not the other way around.

Although Cameron and Wisher never made any money from their first film, Cameron had made an important discovery. He was destined to make movies. There was

To create realistic underwater scenes for the deep-sea thriller *The Abyss*, Cameron built two huge "aquadomes" from the remains of an abandoned power plant.

nothing else he'd rather do, and nothing would stand in his way.

He quit his trucking job and headed over to Roger Corman's New World Pictures to beg for a job—any job—in movies.

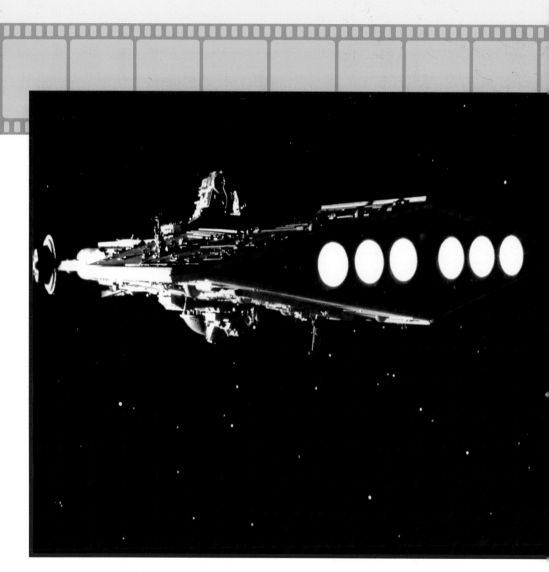

Breaking into the film business wasn't easy for Cameron. He had hoped to start as a special effects cameraman, but instead had to settle for miniature model builder for the 1980 film, *Battle Beyond the Stars*.

Chapter 3

Electrified Maggots

JAMES CAMERON KNEW finding a job in the movie business would be difficult, but not impossible. For one thing, filmmaking is one of the few professions that does not require a college degree. Kenna McHugh, author of *Breaking into Film*, explains:

> A college education is not a prerequisite for working in films. Of course, some of the people hired by studios are college graduates, but some haven't even finished high school. As one professional puts it, " . . . you don't have to be educated in a formal school. You can learn the business by doing."

Often, aspiring filmmakers, especially screenwriters, start out as freelancers who "work for hire," meaning they do a job and get paid for it, but do not work full-time for a movie studio. Then there are interns, typically college students or recent graduates, who work for free because they hope the experience and exposure they are getting will be their ticket into the business. Other aspiring filmmakers accept entry level employment in any department, no matter how unglamorous, hoping to get noticed and promoted.

That's exactly how Roger Corman, founder of New World Pictures, broke into the business.

In 1949, Corman was hired by Twentieth Century Fox to work in the mailroom. Corman saw this as an opportunity to familiarize himself with script writing and studio executives. Before he delivered scripts to his superiors, he would read the scripts and think of ways to improve them. Then, while delivering the script, he would engage executives in conversation, hoping for the chance to offer recommendations. It worked. Corman's insights impressed his superiors, and he was quickly promoted to story analyst.

Two years later, Corman resigned from Fox, returned to school for a while, then became a literary agent. By 1955, he was producing, writing, and directing "B movies," meaning low budget (and usually low quality) films hastily produced and targeted to specific audiences, usually teenagers.

Over the next 16 years, Corman made dozens of movies, some of which were shot in only three days on leftover sets discarded by larger productions. His specialty became gothic horror movies, such as a series of films based on Edgar Allan Poe's short stories, including *The Masque of the Red Death.*

In 1970, he started his own production company, New World Pictures, which eventually became a training ground for rising new talent such as directors Francis Ford Coppola and Martin Scorsese as well as visual effects artists Robert and Dennis Skotak, who eventually won Academy Awards for *Aliens.*

By the time James Cameron applied for a job in 1979, Roger Corman's New World Pictures was trying to capitalize on the success of *Star Wars* by making science fiction movies.

With his spaceship models in tow, Cameron hoped to be hired as a special effects cameraman. Instead, he was offered a job much further down the pecking order: miniature model builder for *Battle Beyond the Stars* (1980), which was just about to begin shooting. He accepted.

Not long into production, Cameron began to get noticed. First, he suggested an improvement for the hero's spaceship, which Roger Corman immediately implemented. Next, Cameron helped director Jimmy T. Murakami solve the problem of shooting realistic live action with miniature models by using large, hand-painted mattes to create the scenery behind the spaceship.

But what really impressed Murakami and Corman was Cameron's knowledge of process photography, a technique whereby live action, models, or miniatures are filmed in front of a transparent screen onto which a previously filmed background scene is projected from the rear. Using this method, directors create the illusion of astronauts, for example, being in outer space or walking on a distant planet when, in fact, they've never

The release of *Star Wars* not only sparked public interest in science fiction movies but also set a new standard for special effects. The film inspired James Cameron to focus his efforts on establishing himself in the movie business. Here, we see the film's two "droids," C3PO and R2D2.

left the studio. Although Cameron had only read about process photography, he never let Murakami or Corman know that. Corman promoted Cameron to process projection supervisor, and Cameron hastily created a front and rear screen projection system to prove his idea would work.

He now had the job he had initially wanted and fantasized about since adolescence: special effects cameraman for a science fiction film. Within four weeks, Cameron was running the visual [special] effects department and had replaced the art director.

Because time was money, Roger Corman wanted his employees to work hard and fast, even if that meant double shifts. Cameron thrived in this "boot camp" atmosphere and often worked triple shifts, all the while learning everything he could about making movies. Years later, he recalled that working for New World Pictures was "like being air-dropped into a battle zone. It was the best, fastest, strongest injection into filmmaking I could have gotten."

He became friends with Gale Anne Hurd, a production assistant and graduate of Stanford University, who resigned from New World Pictures in 1982 to form her own production company. It was Hurd who would later agree to produce Cameron's first screenplay, *The Terminator*.

After *Battle Beyond the Stars*, Cameron's next assignment was to create realistic special effects for John Carpenter's film, *Escape from New York* (1981). Carpenter was already famous for his independent, but enormously popular, horror film, *Halloween*, released in 1978 and starring Jamie Lee Curtis. Cameron, now director of special effects photography, was excited to be working with him.

The setting for the film, *Escape from New York*, is New York City, 1997. The entire city has been turned into a maximum-security prison from which there is no escape. When the president's plane accidentally crashes in Manhattan, a war hero and convict, played by Kurt Russell, is sent on a mission to rescue the president before he is killed by "inmates."

John Carpenter asked Cameron to create a simulated, computerized three-dimensional grid map of downtown Manhattan for the control panel of Russell's futuristic glider, which Russell pilots to the top of the World Trade Center. Carpenter wanted the audience to have the illusion that they were flying over Manhattan with Russell, so Carpenter planned a full screen shot of whatever Cameron could come up with. Computer technology for creating such an effect had not been invented yet, so Cameron relied on his prior success with models.

Using cardboard and black paint, Cameron built a miniature model of downtown Manhattan, then outlined the skyscrapers in Day-Glo paint. Moving his camera slowly through the three-dimensional buildings, he was able to create exactly what Carpenter wanted: a computerized, three-dimensional grid map of a New York City block at night.

Carpenter was thrilled with the results: "Jim Cameron's work just knocked me on my ass. I assigned him something I knew was impossible to do, and he did it with a brilliant simplicity and dedication to achievement."

Then came *Galaxy of Terror* (1981), a science fiction thriller about space explorers landing on a distant planet where their worst fears, literally, come true.

Initially, Cameron wore two hats, that of production designer and special effects supervisor. Cameron was in

Cameron relied on his experience as a model builder to create a grim futuristic setting for John Carpenter's film, *Escape from New York*. In the film, New York City has been turned into a maximum-security prison.

charge of designing the sets, miniatures, and costumes. A few weeks into production, however, Cameron convinced Corman to let him try second unit direction, or directing a few short scenes.

As second unit director, Cameron had to direct a scene in which a dismembered arm is covered with crawling mealworms posing as maggots. Unfortunately, the mealworms were too tranquil and wouldn't cooperate. Always the inventor and problem-solver, Cameron decided to "motivate" the maggots with an electrical charge, unaware that two Italian film producers were on the set seeking a director for the sequel to *Piranha*, a low budget horror film produced by New World in 1978.

Cameron remembers the incident as a comical turning point in his directing career:

> [The arm] is supposed to be covered with maggots. And they've got it covered with this tub of mealworms. You can buy them in pet stores; they're feed for fish, fairly innocuous little creatures. They're pretty law-abiding; they don't do much. They're supposed to writhe around, but they just sat there. So I ran some hidden electrical wires to give them a jolt. I called "Action!" and a technician, hidden from view, threw the juice. The worms started moving like crazy. I say, "Okay, that's good. Cut." The technician pulls the plug and the worms stop. I turn around and these two producers are just gaping. I guess they figured out that if I could get a performance out of mealworms, I should be okay with actors, so they offered me the film.

Before *Galaxy of Terror* was finished, Cameron was on his way to Jamaica to begin directing *Piranha II: The Spawning*. He was 26 years old and very optimistic.

His optimism turned to pessimism, however, when he immediately encountered several problems. First, the script was terrible, mostly because the premise itself was so idiotic: scantily-clad young people being terrorized by flying piranha. Second, the Italian film crew did not speak English. Third, there was no money for special effects. To create the illusion of flying piranhas, Cameron was expected to use baskets of rubber piranhas which crew members simply threw through the air.

Worst of all, Italian producer Ovidio G. Assonitis exercised complete control over the project, often showing up with last minute revisions to the script a few hours before shooting. And once scenes were filmed, Cameron was banned from the editing process.

In short, Cameron's first professional directing experience was a disaster, and he was terminated about 12 days into the shoot. He now chuckles about the experience, saying, "I did not get along very well with the producer. We had irreconcilable creative differences and he unceremoniously fired me."

According to film critic Christopher Heard, the story does not end there. After the film was finished, without Cameron's input, and Cameron realized his name would still appear as director in the film's credits, he was furious. The last thing he wanted was to be associated with such a ridiculous film.

He flew to Rome to confront Assonitis, who told Cameron there was nothing he could do. Supposedly, Cameron believed otherwise and decided to take drastic action. Heard writes that Cameron repeatedly broke into the editing room over several nights and recut the footage to his satisfaction. Although Cameron was eventually discovered, no charges were filed. Assonitis simply recut the film back to its original format and released it two years later in 1983.

Cameron's first job as a director lasted only 12 days. After clashing with the Italian producers of horror film *Piranha 2: The Spawning*, Cameron was fired. But that didn't stop him from flying to Rome and trying to re-edit the film to his satisfaction.

After his confrontation with Assonitis, Cameron stayed in Rome for a while, sick, depressed, and out of money. Although Cameron has said in interviews that the idea of a futuristic hit man for *Terminator* just "came to me," movie fans and critics believe Cameron was inspired to write the screenplay for *Terminator* during this time. Cameron acknowledges his time in Rome was a dark period for him and that no one in the movie business would return his calls.

According to Cameron folklore, Cameron, racked with fever, had a terrifying nightmare. One version says Cameron dreamed of a robotic man chasing him; Heard writes that Cameron dreamed of "a metal skeleton dragging itself across the floor using kitchen knives." Cameron, himself, has been quoted as saying: "I had these images of this metallic death figure coming out of the fire."

Apparently, Cameron awoke from one of these terrifying dreams and wrote down everything he remembered.

The Terminator was born.

The now-famous *Terminator* starring Arnold Schwarzenegger is among James Cameron's most impressive creations. Cameron wrote the screenplay, supervised the special effects, and directed the film.

Chapter 4

"I'll Be Back"

FILMMAKING IS A creative, collaborative process. It is creative because every movie begins with an idea conceived in someone's imagination. It is collaborative because many, many people work together. And it is a process because those same people follow a series of steps to bring the creative idea to life on the screen.

An important player in this process is the writer. Writers turn their ideas into screenplays (plays for the screen), and then sell them to producers who will, with the help of a studio, turn them into movies. Screenplays can be completely original ideas, like Cameron's *Terminator*, or they can be *adapted* screenplays, in other words, screenplays based on existing books or plays.

In writing a screenplay, the author creates characters, plot, and dialog. The more popular the screenwriter, the more likely she is to sell her screenplays and earn the money she desires. Because *The Terminator* was James Cameron's first screenplay, he knew selling it would not be easy. So he cut a deal. A producer could have *The Terminator* screenplay for just one dollar if Cameron would be allowed to direct the film. Gale Anne Hurd, who had worked with Cameron at New World Pictures and was now running Pacific West Productions, agreed.

The producer is another key player in the filmmaking process. Producers are employed by movie studios to find and develop material, hire and assist screenwriters, arrange for studio financing, and oversee the release of the film so it can be seen in theaters across the country or around the world.

Movie studios have additional responsibilities, such as meeting government regulations, housing cast and crew on and off the set, providing transportation, providing film editing and recording studios, and marketing and distributing the finished product.

A third major player in the process is the director. Directors essentially bring the screenplay to life by overseeing all the technical and artistic components of the movie, beginning with cast auditions and set location, and then rehearsals, scenery, costumes, choreography, visual effects, and music.

In the book, *Breaking into Film*, famous Hollywood director Elia Kazan describes what it takes to be a director:

What kind of a person must a director train himself to be? What qualities does he need? Here are a few: A construction gang foreman. . . . a hypnotist . . . a poet. . . . an outfielder . . . a trader in a Baghdad bazaar . . . an animal trainer . . . a mother . . . a father . . . a jewel thief . . . and a PR [public relations] man. . . .

Directors must be resourceful and multitalented. They must be capable of solving miniscule and mammoth problems at a moment's notice. They must be able to inspire and intimidate their cast, crew, and even studio executives. They must have vision and uncompromising faith in themselves and the project. The screenwriter may be the engine of a car, and the producer may own the car, but the director drives the car where she wants it to go.

Finally, there is the production manager. He spends the money to keep the car running by overseeing crew, travel, casting, and equipment expenses.

When these four individuals unite to make a movie, they work together in three stages: preproduction, production, and postproduction.

The preproduction stage is the planning stage. During this time, the producer, art director, location scout, and casting director begin to lay the foundation for the film. While the location scout explores possible locations for shooting, the art director tries to visualize set construction, scenery, props, and costumes. The casting director organizes auditions or approaches the agents of the actors already being considered. Money is budgeted for all of these expenses plus visual effects costs, if necessary.

The next phase is production (sometimes called principal photography). This is when shooting starts.

Creating "movie magic" is a team effort. The director must be able to work effectively with many skilled professionals—both behind and in front of the camera—to make a film successful.

The director, actors, cinematographers (movie photographers), sound engineers, and visual effects technicians work to create "movie magic."

Actors work from a script, the section of the screenplay they are rehearsing at the moment. Cameron refers to a script as a "proposal" because it presents certain ideas which actors, music, lighting, visual effects, editing and the director all bring to life.

Visual or special effects technicians must be particularly imaginative and resourceful. To some extent, they must be carpenters, electricians, plumbers, and electronics and animation experts. If a screenplay calls for an explosion, earthquake, or even dinosaurs, visual effects technicians must make it happen.

Because a budget is established in preproduction, the producer and production manager strive to keep production expenses in line. If a director starts to spend too much money, like James Cameron often does, the producer gets nervous. Likewise, the movie studio which has agreed to make and release the film, wants assurances that production is going well and not exceeding the budget.

Often, however, problems or delays in production are unavoidable. Scenes are rewritten to accommodate a particular set or prop. Scenes are delayed because a stunt expert isn't ready. And scenes are thrown out altogether because they just aren't working.

During production, conflicts often erupt between directors and their producers and movie studios. This is because directors view their work as an art form, a creative endeavor which is entitled to change. Conversely, producers and movie studios view filmmaking as a business. They are more concerned with getting a return on their investment than they are producing a quality film. For this reason, Cameron is fond of calling producers and movie studio executives "suits" and "bean counters" as opposed to artists like himself.

The last phase of filmmaking is postproduction. This is when the movie receives its finishing touches. Film editors study the footage to determine which shots should stay and which shots should go. Sometimes the sequence of shots changes. Other times entire scenes are eliminated. Dialog is cut.

Screenwriters and directors are accustomed to seeing parts of their work sacrificed. Cameron is quite philosophical and pragmatic about the process, saying: "I do not allow myself to fall in love with words. I fall in love with performances and images, and I protect them through the cutting process [only] when they are worthy."

During postproduction, the film is also edited for sound. Sound effects editors and audio recording engineers work together to add prerecorded and live sound effects as well as background music to create the appropriate mood. Slowly, the film begins to take shape.

If film and sound editing do not go well, directors may return to the production phase to make substantial changes. Producers and studios become very unhappy when this occurs. Returning to production means a delayed release date and additional expenses the studio may never recoup. Time is money to movie studios.

If the film is pronounced ready for release, the studio's advertising and marketing departments spring into action. Press releases are written for newspapers, television, and radio stations. Short biographies of the director and cast are made available, and the principal actors begin promoting the film on talk shows. A "trailer," or coming attraction, starts running in theaters.

Like all movies, *Terminator* started with an idea. James Cameron envisioned a story about a cyborg—half-man, half-machine—who is sent back in time to change the course of history.

Cameron sketched some scenes first to create a storyboard, which directors often use to help them visualize certain scenes before the cameras start rolling. One sketch was of a cyborg pursuing an injured woman by pulling himself across a floor using a kitchen knife, supposedly just like Cameron's dream in Rome.

Together, Cameron (who was now separated from his first wife) and Gale Anne Hurd polished *The Terminator* screenplay. In the story, a "terminator" is sent from the future to 1984 Los Angeles to kill Sarah Connor, the mother of an unborn son who eventually grows up to lead a resistance movement against machines which dominate the earth after a nuclear holocaust. To protect the mother, the resistance sends back Reese, a soldier who tells the frightened and incredulous Sarah she will become a warrior in her own right—if she can stay alive.

After Hurd agreed to produce the film, she had to find a studio. Hurd sent the screenplay to several studios, but the reaction was always the same: no. Then Hurd tried British producer John Daly at Hemdale Pictures. He read the screenplay and agreed to meet Cameron.

According to Christopher Heard, Cameron knew he would only have one chance to pitch the movie. So he dressed up an actor friend of his to play the Terminator for the interview. The actor slicked his hair back, put pieces of gold foil over his teeth, and wore a ripped shirt, leather jacket, and boots. Cameron applied fake cuts to his friend's head, and off they went.

The award-winning husband-and-wife team of writer-director James Cameron and producer Gale Anne Hurd created movie hits like *The Terminator*, *Aliens*, and *The Abyss*.

Daly was impressed, not only with the Terminator performance, but also with Cameron's storyboard. He and Cameron struck a deal: Hemdale Pictures would make the movie, but shooting would not begin for another two and half years.

Meanwhile, Cameron decided to sharpen his screen-writing skills by working as a "script doctor" on existing screenplays, and as a ghost writer for other screenplays, which means he received no credit for the work even though he was paid for his services. He also served as design consultant for *Android* (1982).

Word spread that Cameron was a decent screenwriter and, almost simultaneously, he was offered the chance to write two sequels: one to *First Blood*, released in 1982 and starring Sylvester Stallone, and another to Ridley Scott's *Alien*, released in 1979. Shortly there-after, Cameron was notified that Hemdale Pictures would begin shooting *The Terminator* in about six months and Orion Pictures would distribute the film.

Most screenwriters would be intimidated by the daunt-ing task of writing two screenplays in a few months' time, but Cameron has always been very methodical and systematic when it comes to writing. He also thrives under pressure.

Immediately, he looked at a calendar and figured out how many days and working hours he had to finish each project before directing *The Terminator*. Then he divided the number of working hours available by the number of hours he needed to write a page to calculate the number of pages he would be able to write on a daily and weekly basis.

Despite being so organized, Cameron admits he never looks forward to writing. He once told a reporter that writing was the most frightening step in the making of a film: "I've been to the South Pole, flown barrel rolls in a supersonic jet fighter, and been to the bottom of the ocean in a submarine, but the most terrifying thing I've ever faced is the blank page."

Like most writers, Cameron never writes a great screenplay on the first try. He incubates or daydreams an interesting plot first, "nibbling at its edges" and taking notes. Then he writes an outline, one line for each scene. From the outline he writes a "scriptment," a long, detailed narration which depicts every important scene the way Cameron envisions it on the big screen. He describes the process this way:

> I start sticking words in the characters who are still mannequins, forcing them to move and walk like animated corpses . . . Slowly, their movements become more human, and their skin gets pink with the flow of blood...The characters begin to say things in their own words. By the end of this period I'm writing 10 pages a day.

Ultimately, these scriptments must be chopped to a manageable length. Heard explains: "One page of a standard screenplay usually translates to one minute of screen time, so these first drafts must then be tightly edited. All the fat is stripped away until only the meat of the story remains."

During such a "fragile stage of creation," Cameron tries not to worry about whether his film will be a financial success, believing such anxiety is "the death of art" or counter-productive to the creative process.

While writing the screenplay for the sequel to *First Blood*, Cameron wanted to further develop the character of John Rambo, the ostracized and misunderstood Vietnam War veteran who vents his frustration by wreaking havoc. In *Rambo: First Blood II*, Cameron emphasized Rambo's courage and self-sacrifice by having him return to Vietnam on a mission to rescue prisoners of war.

Stallone accepted Cameron's screenplay, but made

While waiting to begin work on *The Terminator*, Cameron wrote the screenplay for *Rambo: First Blood Part II*, starring Sylvester Stallone. Despite some disagreements between star and screenwriter, the film was a huge success.

revisions which displeased Cameron. One revision was to eliminate a sidekick character, who, Stallone felt, had the better lines. Released in the summer of 1985, *Rambo: First Blood II* was an instant box office success even though movie critics panned it.

Simultaneous to working on *Rambo: First Blood II*, Cameron was also working on the screenplay for *Aliens*, the sequel to Ridley Scott's *Alien* (1979). When producers Walter Hill and David Giler first approached Cameron to write the screenplay, they had just one requirement for the plot: "Ripley and soldiers."

Cameron liked the idea immediately, saying: "I thought the concept of grunts in space was wonderful. So I took that idea and all the elements of the first [*Alien*] that I liked and thought would be worth retaining, and from there the story crystallized very quickly."

Hill and Giler liked what Cameron showed them and offered him the opportunity to direct the film. Cameron agreed on the conditions that they would wait for him to finish directing *The Terminator* and that Gale Anne Hurd would be hired as producer. Twentieth Century Fox and Brandywine Pictures budgeted $18 million for the project.

Meanwhile, *The Terminator* was now in preproduction, and the first order of business was to select the cast. Hemdale Pictures wanted Arnold Schwarzenegger to be the hero and former football star O.J. Simpson to be the Terminator. But Cameron had other ideas. He convinced Schwarzenegger he would be perfect as the Terminator by telling him the star of the film was the villain, not the hero, and then cast Michael Biehn as Reese and Linda Hamilton as Sarah Connor.

Schwarzenegger was less than enthusiastic at first and reportedly complained, "I don't know what kind of crazy movie this is. They're from outer space and they are shooting each other. They shoot each other every minute. It's crazy."

After casting his actors, Cameron hired visual effects and makeup wizard Stan Winston to create realistic human prosthetics devices for the scene in which the

Cameron brought his full knowledge of special effects to *The Terminator*, creating a high-energy hit that bridged the gap between science fiction and fast-paced action.

Terminator repairs his own arm in front of a mirror. In another gruesome scene, the Terminator removes a bloody eyeball and drops it into a sink. To hide his mechanical eye inside a gaping socket, the cyborg sports sunglasses.

Cameron's special effects team also built a 100-pound, life-size animatronic (remote-controlled puppet) of the Terminator's skeleton and an identical two-foot robot, both of which were chrome-plated and used in the last scenes when the Terminator's body is incinerated and then crushed by a hydraulic press.

Cameron employed stop-motion photography to film some of the larger animatronic's movements. Stop-motion (also referred to as stop-action) photography has been around since the early twentieth century and is the predecessor of modern day animation. The technique creates the illusion of inanimate objects moving by themselves by camera operators shooting frames one at a time so that in between camera shots the object can be moved ever so slightly. When the film is projected back at normal speed, or 24 frames per second, the object looks like it is moving all by itself.

During production, Cameron began to develop a reputation for being a perfectionist—and crazy. Yet he never asked his cast or crew to do something he couldn't do himself and often went to great lengths to prove it could be done, including dangerous physical stunts.

Despite its shoestring budget of about $4 million, *Terminator* pleased movie fans and critics alike. David J. Skal, author of *The Monster Show: A Cultural History of Horror,* likened Schwarzenegger's Terminator to a modern day Frankenstein. And Arnold Schwarzenegger became an instant star with his infamous line, "I'll be back."

Movie director John Badham praised Cameron's talent and persistence, saying Cameron made *Terminator* for "25 cents and it looks terrific!"

Alan Karp, writing for *Box Office Magazine,* said:

"Despite its strange premise and cartoonish (but competent) special effects, *The Terminator* is a humorously suspenseful thriller, which makes the most of what it's got."

After his devastating experience directing *Piranha II: The Spawning*, Cameron was indeed "back."

Cameron poses with producer and second wife Gale Anne Hurd and the cast of *The Abyss*. From the start of filming, Cameron insisted on strict safety and training procedures for his actors and crew.

"Life's Abyss and Then You Dive"

INSPIRED BY THE success of his first screenplay, *The Terminator*, Cameron was now ready to tackle the challenge of directing *Aliens*, the sequel to *Alien* (1979), directed by British filmmaker Ridley Scott and starring Sigourney Weaver. Once again, Gale Anne Hurd would be the producer.

Alien is about futuristic space mining engineers aboard a spaceship called the Nostromo. While responding to an SOS signal on planet LV426, crew members bring aboard a vicious, intelligent life form which has attached itself to the face of a crew member—right through the protective glass on his space helmet. The alien reproduces by depositing an egg down the throat of a human host, who immediately slips into a coma while the egg incubates in the stomach. When the creature is ready to be born, the host's stomach explodes.

After the alien hatches from the stomach of the Nostromo crew member, it scurries off and hides in the ventilation system of the ship until it is large enough to begin killing off people one by one. When the crew attempts to injure or kill the alien, it bleeds acid. To make matters worse, there is a traitor on board: a menacing robot, resembling a human, who is under orders by "the company" to protect all newly discovered lifeforms for possible use in biological warfare—no matter what the cost to ship and crew.

After fending off this evil robot, sole survivor Lt. Ripley (Weaver) eventually outwits the alien and ejects it from a shuttle craft which she hopes to ride to safety. The movie ends with Ripley putting herself into hibernation until she and her ship can be rescued.

Although *Alien* was only moderately successful at the box office, critics liked the film, so Cameron wanted the sequel to be just as praiseworthy. In Cameron's film, the story begins where *Alien* leaves off. Fifty-seven years after putting herself to sleep in the shuttlecraft, Ripley is rescued by a salvage ship owned by the same company which owned her previous ship. Company representative Carter Burke (Paul Reiser) and others are skeptical when Ripley tells them what the alien did to her crew so many years before, especially since American colonists and scientists have been living on planet LV426 for the past 20 years without incident.

Ripley's story is suddenly taken seriously when the inhabitants of LV426 seem to be in trouble. Marines are dispatched to lend assistance, and Burke persuades Ripley to go as a civilian advisor. Here is where Cameron improves upon the original storyline's elements.

In Scott's film, Ripley is a loner. However, in *Aliens*, she develops two meaningful relationships: one with marine corporal Hicks (Michael Biehn); and another with a little girl nicknamed "Newt," (Carrie Henn), whose parents have been killed, along with everyone else, by the time Ripley and the marines arrive. Almost everyone in the film is a compelling or likable character, including the robot who becomes a hero when he rescues Ripley and Newt at the last minute, enabling Ripley to battle the alien queen from inside a power loader (mechanical lifter) and eject her from an air lock on board the marine's spaceship.

Like *Terminator, Aliens* is an illustration of Cameron's fascination with science fiction, strong women, and machinery. Not only are both movies sci-fi thrillers, but they also feature independent, heroic women using heavy machinery to defeat the enemy.

Cameron's determination to create realistic special effects is also evident in *Aliens*. Cameron hired Stan Winston again to oversee the creation of the aliens as well as other important visual effects of the film. Sometimes the aliens were actually stunt persons and dancers who wore black leotards, fitted with lightweight foam pieces to simulate the aliens' bodies and spider-like arms and legs. Other aliens were expendable 8-foot-tall puppets which could be destroyed during certain scenes. Just like in *Terminator*, two versions of the alien queen were created: a full-sized mechanical puppet, this time

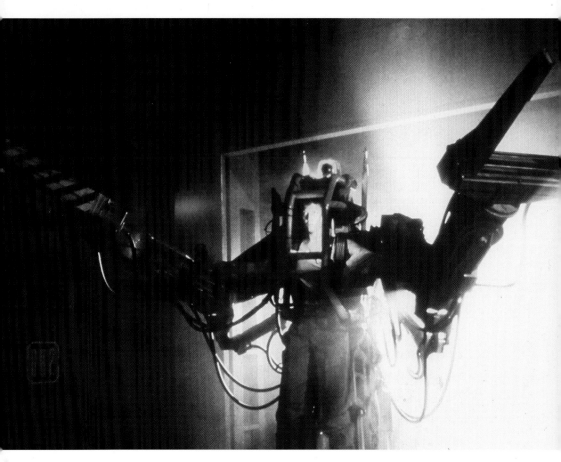

In creating *Aliens* (the sequel to Ridley Scott's *Alien*), Cameron further developed the character of Ripley (played by Sigourney Weaver) while creating even more terrifying special effects.

operated by two stunt persons inside; and a smaller puppet operated by remote control.

Cameron did not use stop-motion photography this time, however, believing it was not realistic enough for "organic creatures." And rather than rely on matte paintings, which he felt were too artificial, Cameron relied on front and rear screen projection techniques, which he had mastered at New World Pictures. He shot the scenes of the aliens' nesting place in an old power station in West London.

For the final battle between Ripley and the queen in the airlock of the space ship, Cameron wanted close-up shots to be very realistic, so he hung the mechanical queen from invisible wires. The power loader, under which the queen is ultimately trapped and ejected into space, was made of light plastic capable of withstanding all the battering the final scene entails. This sequence alone took five days to shoot.

Just as Cameron had hoped, *Aliens* was a box office hit, earning more than $80 million. It also received seven Oscar nominations, include a Best Actress nomination for Signourney Weaver, the first time an actress was nominated for a science fiction film. Stan Winston won an Oscar for Best Visual Effects.

Nevertheless, critics' reviews were mixed. *Variety* magazine described *Aliens* as being a "very worthy follow-up to Ridley Scott's 1979 sci-fi shocker." The *New York Times* said the film was "a touch less innovative than its predecessor." And famous movie critic Roger Ebert, of the *Chicago Sun Times*, had this to say:

> The movie made me feel bad. It filled me with feelings of unease and disquiet and anxiety . . . I was drained. I'm not sure if *Aliens* is what we mean by entertainment. Yet I have to be accurate about this movie: It is a superb example of filmmaking craft.

Despite the mixed reviews, Cameron was thrilled with the attention *Aliens* was getting, mostly because he feels that Hollywood does not take science fiction movies seriously. Given society's dependence on technology, some of which originated in the minds of science fiction writers years ago, Cameron wonders why this genre is never given the respect it deserves.

"I love science fiction," he says. "We live in a sci-fi world. We live in a world that has been transformed in the last 15 years by a microchip. And we are living in a world that no one could have imagined, and we have adapted to it."

In addition to being happy about the success of *Aliens*, Cameron was also happy in his personal life. A year before *Aliens* was released, he had married producer Gale Anne Hurd.

Today, *Aliens* fans can watch a special edition of the film offering 17 extra minutes of footage boasting more "intricately etched characters."

After the success of *Aliens*, Fox studio executives were eager to work with James Cameron again, especially when he pitched the idea for his next movie. Cameron's idea was this: the ocean depths are just as mysterious, awe-inspiring, and frightening as outer space. If America sends astronauts into space using state-of-the-art technology, why not make a film about sending people on a mission to the deepest part of the ocean floor? The movie would be called *The Abyss*.

According to Cameron's biographer, Christopher Heard, the premise for the movie came to Cameron after a high school class trip to a science exhibition in Buffalo, New York, where he first learned about breathing liguid oxygen underwater. He was only 17 years old.

Sometime later, while bored in biology class, Cameron decided to write a short story titled "The Abyss." In the story, Cameron originally envisioned an advanced race of underwater creatures whose peaceful way of life comes in conflict with potentially self-destructive humans living above them.

As a high school student, Cameron could never have predicted his short story would one day be the premise for a $50 million motion picture. On the other hand, Cameron believes that everything he writes is from cumulative experiences and ideas that he has nurtured over time.

"I waste nothing," he says. "I am like the Plains Indians, who would kill a buffalo for the meat but then use every other part for some practical purpose or another. I can say quite honestly . . . that I tinkered with the story of 'The Abyss' that I wrote in biology class, when I was 17, from the day I wrote it until the day the special edition laserdisc was released."

Cameron was also inspired to make *The Abyss* when he saw a 1987 National Geographic Explorer documentary about Dr. Robert Ballard's discovery of the *Titanic* two years before. To find the wreck, Ballard had towed an underwater camera which sent images to the ship via a fiber-optic umbilical cord. Ballard had then explored the *Titanic* in a miniature submersible, using a remote-controlled camera nicknamed Jason Jr. That same documentary would also be the inspiration for Cameron's *Titanic* released 10 years later.

The Abyss, starring Ed Harris, Mary Elizabeth Mastrantonio, and Michael Biehn, opens with an American submarine in trouble after colliding with a mysterious NTI (non-terrestrial intelligence). The Navy organizes a rescue mission and asks crew members of Deepcore, a deep-sea oil-drilling rig, to be a diving support team. Oil rig foreman Bud Brigman (Harris) is reluctant, but agrees when the Navy tells him the rescue is a matter of national security because the submarine is carrying Trident missiles. Lindsay Brigman, Bud's ex-wife and designer of Deepcore, lends assistance as does an uptight, by-the-book Navy SEAL lieutenant named

The deep-sea thriller *The Abyss*, starring Ed Harris and Mary Elizabeth Mastrantonio, required Cameron to utilize special effects using blue-screen technology, where actors would have to pretend to be interacting with the sea creatures, which were added to the film later.

Coffey (Biehn). Meanwhile, tropical storm Hurricane Frederick heads toward the oil rig.

On the rescue mission, Bud's crew and NAVY SEALs encounter a series of obstacles. First, Coffey begins to suffer from high-pressure nervous disorder and can't be trusted. Second, Hurricane Frederick topples a huge steel crane linking the Explorer, Deepcore's topside support vessel, with Deepcore; as the crane sinks, it drags Deepcore along the ocean floor to the brink of an underwater trough or abyss. Third, all communication and air supply provided to Deepcore crew members from the Explorer is severed. Finally, Coffey, now completely deranged, locks up the Deepcore crew so that he and his SEALs can accomplish their mission alone.

But Deepcore has help: friendly, watery beings who make their presence known first to Lindsay, and then others, including Coffey. After his encounter with the aliens, Coffey panics and decides to detonate a nuclear warhead strapped to a submersible, which he boards to escape Bud and Lindsay in an underwater chase scene. When Coffey is killed, the armed warhead sinks into the abyss, and Bud descends to its depths to disarm it. Breathing liquid oxygen and going deeper than no man has ever gone, Bud begins to exhibit the same symptoms of high-pressure nervous disorder that plagued Coffey. All seems lost until the angelic-looking aliens come to Bud's rescue after he sends a computerized message to Lindsay, saying: "I love you wife."

Cameron was determined to shoot *The Abyss* almost entirely underwater, so he created two aquadomes out of an abandoned nuclear power plant in South Carolina. The concrete shell of the reactor became the main tank and held 7.5 million gallons of water. A nearby smaller tank held 2.5 million gallons. Gigantic tarps were kept over both tanks to create the illusion of dark, deep seawater.

Before shooting could begin, the cast and crew had to undergo intensive training on underwater safety.

Actors had to learn how to dive and swim wearing heavy scuba gear and helmets equipped with speaker systems. They often rehearsed for 11-hour intervals underwater, reading scripts laminated in plastic. To minimize unnecessary trips to the surface for oxygen tank refills, Cameron installed an underwater filling station. At the end of a long day, everyone had to decompress, which means allowing the body to adjust gradually to less water pressure before attempting to swim to the surface.

Cameron's insistence on following safety procedures bordered on the tyrannical. Perhaps he believed the lines he had written for Bud Brigman actually referred to Cameron himself: "When it comes to the safety of these people, there's me and then there's God, understand?"

There were other problems as well: underwater lights malfunctioning; weather conditions; equipment damage; and the stress brought on by working in such a claustrophobic environment. On more than one occasion, actor Ed Harris and others expressed concern over the scenes they were expected to shoot underwater. In fact, some staff members good-naturedly protested Cameron's high expectations of them by wearing t-shirts that read: "Life's Abyss and Then You Dive."

In his defense, Cameron is very philosophical about his role as a director: "I believe in having the same intensity on the set one would have in a championship basketball game or Super Bowl . . . So I'm pretty high energy on the set. I'm usually fighting a schedule, that given the difficulty of what we're doing, is tight . . . There is no room for compromise."

Ian Spelling, writing for *Starlog Magazine,* observes that directing can be a lonely task, even if hundreds of

One of the most exciting challenges in creating *The Abyss* was make water come to life. Cameron employed a special effects company to create computer-animated images that would make the film's "pseudopods" seem real.

people surround the director every day. Cameron agrees:

> It is a very strange situation. Any director who claims he made a movie by himself is an idiot. [But] there basically must be . . . someone to say, 'Do it this way.' It doesn't matter if they're right or wrong. The trick in directing is probably the trick in any operation where you have that responsibility. You make a decision, right or wrong, and you follow it through without equivocation, or else you lose the crew's faith.

Shooting *The Abyss* required photographic techniques rarely attempted underwater before, namely rear-screen and blue-screen projection work, and special effects such as photo-realistic animation. Cameron was already familiar with rear-screen projection, having practiced this while at New World Pictures. He was also experienced with blue-screen photography, the technique of filming a subject in front of a blue screen instead of the real background, which allows the subject to be added digitally to another scene later—for example, in front of a miniature set or previously filmed footage. In this way, for example, special effects technicians create the illusion of someone flying over the Grand Canyon when, in reality, the actress is pretending to fly in front of a blue screen. But few filmmakers had attempted rear-screen and blue-screen projection underwater, so Cameron asked his brother, Mike, an aeronautical engineer, to help coordinate underwater lighting and photography.

Likewise, Cameron realized that because his visual effects expertise was primarily puppetry, painted mattes, and miniature models, he would need help with photo-realistic animation. So he hired special effects expert Steve Johnson and George Lucas's special effects company, Industrial Lights and Magic (ILM), to create the "irregularly shaped, organic-looking creatures or 'pseudopods'" inhabiting the abyss.

Cameron wanted these creatures to be snake-like, translucent, and made entirely of sea water. Powerful, yet friendly, they had to be able to resemble human faces, yet revert to sea water if touched or threatened.

To accomplish this, ILM technicians created realistic three-dimensional animation using computer graphics and software which made it possible for ILM techncians to resize and color-correct digitized images. However, it was the combination of live action and computer graphics which made the special effects in *The Abyss* so astounding. The 75-second scene, wherein an alien humorously mimics Lindsay's and Bud's facial expressions, required 20 technicians and eight months of work, but won the film an Oscar for Best Visual Effects. More importantly, *The Abyss* pioneered special effects technology used in later films, such as *Total Recall* (1990), *Terminator 2: Judgment Day* (1991), *Jurassic Park* (1993), and *Forrest Gump* (1994).

Unfortunately, *The Abyss* ran longer than Twentieth Century Fox wanted. Cameron was told to shorten the film by 28 minutes. To everyone's surprise, he cut spectacular tidal wave sequences that had been very difficult to shoot. (Fox had recommended cutting love scenes between Bud and Lindsay.) Today, movie fans can watch the tidal wave scenes in an uncut version of the movie on DVD titled *The Abyss: The Special Edition.*

The Abyss was released in the summer of 1989, and, like *Aliens,* the critics' reviews were mixed. Unlike *Aliens*, *The Abyss* did not rake in huge profits, coming too late in the summer to compete with other blockbusters like *Batman* and *Lethal Weapon 2*. Even worse, the strain of making *The Abyss* had taken a toll on Cameron's marriage to Gale Anne Hurd. The couple divorced in 1989, and Cameron married action film director Kathryn Bigelow that same year.

The following year, Cameron started his own production company. He named it Lightstorm Entertainment, referring to the special effects in the opening scene of *Terminator*. By creating Lightstorm Entertainment, Cameron hoped to have more control over future films. The company was housed in an industrial media center on the outskirts of Los Angeles.

Cameron based the role of *The Terminator*'s Sarah Connor on his first wife, Sharon. Actress Linda Hamilton, who later became Cameron's fourth wife, jumped at the chance to play Sarah in the film.

"You Can't Scare Me. I Work for James Cameron."

LIKE MANY TALENTED artists, James Cameron knows how to deal with rejection as well as acceptance, and with disappointment as well as success. When *The Abyss* did not earn the accolades that Cameron had hoped for, he threw himself into another project with his friend, William Wisher.

Wisher had helped Cameron make *Xenogenesis*, Cameron's first film and his ticket into New World Pictures. Wisher had also gotten an "additional dialog" credit for a couple of scenes in the original *Terminator* film. Now Cameron wanted Wisher to help him write the sequel to *Terminator*.

Wisher did not need much convincing. He and Cameron spent two weeks brainstorming ideas and acting out possible scenes for the film, storing them in computer files until they felt they had enough to write a treatment (a lengthy rough draft without dialog). Then they split the treatment in two, with Wisher taking the first half and Cameron taking the second.

Before they separated to write by themselves, Cameron and Wisher agreed on several elements: the story would open 12 years after the first one ended; Sarah Connor would be in a mental hospital; and Connor's son John would be saved by a good terminator sent back to kill the bad terminator ordered to kill John.

These elements were somewhat problematic. As Cameron recalls: "The tricky part was having it all make sense to a member of the audience who didn't remember or hadn't seen the first *Terminator*, and therefore I had to create a backstory for [Sarah Connor] . . . The sequel had to be a story about someone who encountered something that nobody else believes." Hence the scene in which Sarah Connor tries to convince psychiatrists that she's not crazy.

Another challenge was to invent a bad Terminator so intimidating he was a match for Arnold Schwarzenegger's good Terminator. Rather than try to top Schwarzenegger's build, Cameron decided the new Terminator would be, according to Christopher Heard, "smaller, faster, and a lot more advanced than his adversary." Both Terminators would still be programmed killing machines—just operating under different orders.

As Cameron and Wisher each wrote their half of the treatment, they traded pages back and forth and continued to brainstorm over the telephone. Cameron told Wisher: "Just make scenes. If it's [expletive], we'll throw it out later."

Before the screenplay was finished, Cameron worried about casting. He felt pretty confident that Arnold Schwarzenegger would want to reprise his role as the Terminator, but Linda Hamilton was another story, especially since the actress was on the verge of accepting a part in another film.

When Cameron approached Hamilton, he explained: "Your son is the target and you are in a mental hospital. The kid teams up with a good Terminator, they break you out of the mental hospital, then you all save the world."

Hamilton was hooked.

Now Cameron had to hook Schwarzenegger for sure. He made plans to travel with Schwarzenegger to the Cannes Film Festival in France, where Carolco Pictures would be announcing upcoming projects at a party and press conference. Carolco Pictures, which had made both *Rambo* movies, had secured the sequel rights to *Terminator* and had offered Cameron the opportunity to write and direct the movie. Cameron's company, Lightstorm Entertainment, would produce the film.

Cameron worked like a "wounded, pregnant wolverine holed up in a cave" to deliver a complete screenplay to Schwarzenegger before the film festival, so Schwarzenegger could decide if he really wanted to do the film. If Schwarzenegger agreed, he and Cameron would announce the project together. Furthermore, the studio had promised Cameron free rein on the film if he could deliver Schwarzenegger.

Cameron vividly remembers his writing frenzy, which ended just as the limousine pulled into his driveway to take him to the airport: "I took [Wisher's] scenes and pasted them in. I worked the last 36 hours straight to finish in time for the plane. The last 25 pages wrote themselves in a non-stop pounding of keys. My fingers were sore."

Schwarzenegger recalls how he read the screenplay from start to finish on the plane: "I couldn't put it down. I handed Jim the script and said, 'I'm in.'"

Carolco Pictures wanted a July 4, 1991 release date, which meant Cameron had only 13 months to deliver the film. First, he had to polish the rough screenplay he had shown Schwarzenegger into a shooting script for preproduction, which began in July 1990. He continued to revise the script up until shooting started in October, and then again through production in January, February, and April, when he wrapped up shooting.

In the editing room, Cameron made more revisions, removing flashback scenes and dialog between and Sarah and Reese (the soldier sent to rescue her in the first film). Cameron believes that just because a scene worked on paper doesn't mean the scene will work on film. The finished product captivated critics and movie fans alike.

Terminator 2: Judgment Day opens in 2029 Los Angeles. As the audience looks at a city in ruins, Sarah Connor's voice explains how a Terminator was sent from the future to kill her in 1984 so that she could not conceive a son who would one day lead a rebellion against machines responsible for a nuclear holocaust. She explains that the Terminator's mission failed and that two more Terminators are now being sent back—one determined to kill her son and another determined to protect him.

The next two scenes depict both Terminators arriving amidst electrical disturbances: the original one played by Schwarzenegger and a T-1000, played by Robert Patrick. Shortly thereafter, the audience meets 12-year-old John Connor (Ed Furlong), who is in foster care because his mother is, presumably, mentally unstable.

Young actor Ed Furlong played 12-year-old John Connor in *Terminator 2: Judgment Day*. In directing *T2*, Cameron had to outdo himself, with even more gripping special effects than in the first film.

At this point, the movie's pace quickens and never stops. The Terminator and T-1000 battle it out time and again as Sarah and John Connor try to stay one step ahead of annihilation. Although John immediately trusts the Terminator, Sarah Connor does not, even though the Terminator tells her the name of the man responsible for creating the technology which eventually enables machines to dominate the world.

The man is Miles Dyson (Joe Morton) and he works for Cyberdyne Systems. Sarah Connor decides to kill Dyson single-handedly, so his ideas will never come to fruition. Before she has a chance to accomplish her mission, John and the Terminator arrive and enlist Dyson's help in destroying any research he has begun which will help the machines later.

With T-1000 in pursuit, John, Sarah, and the Terminator flee to an old steel mill, where the Terminator covers T-1000 in liquid nitrogen, freezing him solid so he can be blasted into pieces with a shotgun. But high temperatures in the steel plant thaw the frozen pieces of T-1000 and he is able to reassemble himself, although not for long. Minutes later, he is destroyed in a vat of steamy, molten steel. The Terminator wants to die with T-1000 to prevent future scientists from discovering the technology which built them, but he is programmed not to self-destruct. So, in a gut-wrenching scene, Sarah lowers the Terminator into the same vat while her son looks on in horror. Mother, son, and audiences are somewhat consoled, however, when the Terminator gives a thumbs-up sign just before completely sinking out of sight.

Cameron knew the special effects he wanted for *Terminator 2* would mean breaking new ground again and, most likely, exceeding his budget. So he teamed up with Stan Winston once more to get the most for his money.

Winston's first assignment was to create a coming attraction which would hint at the Terminator's return in movie theaters across North America. On a budget of $150,000, Winston directed a four-minute trailer showing hundreds of Schwarzenegger-like Terminators being manufactured at an unidentified factory in the future. This way, Terminator fans would be able to accept Schwarzenegger's character

The climax of *T2* occurs when the two Terminators face off in a steel mill.

returning to the screen even though Sarah Connor had crushed him in a hydraulic press 12 years before.

Winston had other challenges. "Jim came up with hundreds of insane, impossible effects which he always does," Winston has said. "There were more effects written in the first two minutes of this movie than the entire first movie."

Industrial Lights and Magic (ILM) was hired to create the most difficult special effect: the silvery, shape-shifting T-1000 cyborg bent on destroying John Connor. The menacing cyborg had to be capable of shifting from hard to liquid metal, from human to machine. As in *The Abyss*, computer-generated imagery (CGI) was used to blend realistic 3-D computer graphics with live action, particularly when the T-1000 morphs from human to liquid metal, then back to human again after surviving a wall of fire. In another spectacular scene at the psychiatric hospital where Sarah Connor is being held, the T-1000's arm becomes a steel blade capable of opening elevator doors.

During production, a cast and crew of thousands descended upon Los Angeles, and, once again, Cameron earned a reputation for being a control freak. According to Hollywood reporter Paula Parisi, Cameron "threatened to fire a crew member who left for the restroom, made his team work through meals, and insulted his crew over a loudspeaker system."

As with *The Abyss*, crew members made up t-shirts which read: "You can't scare me. I work for James Cameron" and "Terminator 3: Not With Me!" Yet reporters like Brian D. Johnson of *Maclean's* often found Cameron good-natured and soft-spoken, albeit shrewd and cautious when it came to answering certain questions about his work. Nevertheless, Cameron was eager to defend himself against charges that he was "an insensitive jock who likes to blow stuff up, burn money, and terrorize anyone who gets in his way."

Cameron will be the first to admit he is intense. His idea of relaxation is riding dirt bikes, scuba diving, and bungee jumping. He has also vacationed at the South Pole. But Cameron sees his intensity as an asset in

Cameron is known for his intensity as a director. Although he admits to being a tough taskmaster with his cast and crew, the commitment and dedication he puts into his films always produce amazing results.

directing, not a detriment. And he does not apologize for being a taskmaster: "It's just part of the working process for me. Some people take it personally and some people don't. The ones who work with me again are the ones who don't . . . I'm harsh on people because I want to inspire them to do their very best. . . . "

Furthermore, Cameron likes to dispel the myth that filmmaking should be a positive experience, involving one big happy family. "It's war," he says.

Still, Cameron has his admirers. Close friend Arnold Schwarzenegger says making movies with Cameron is a terrific experience for an actor:

> Working with Jim Cameron is unique because he is basically everything! He writes the screenplay, he comes up with the concept, he directs the scenes. He wants to do his own lighting and he wants to work the camera himself . . . You see him using the smoke machines and you see him putting on the blood and trying to do your makeup even though the makeup and special effects people have done it already . . . That is why a Jim Cameron movie has that look, that special unique look.

Movie fans agreed that *Terminator 2: Judgment Day* had the right look. Even though the film cost over $100 million to produce, it made more money in less than a week than *The Abyss* had made in its entire run, eventually earning $500 million in box office profits. The film also won the People's Choice Award for Best Film, the MTV Movie Award for Best Action Sequence, and four Oscars for Best Makeup, Best Sound, Best Sound Effects Editing, and Best Visual Effects.

Not nearly as successful, but also released in 1991, was *Point Break*, a film produced by Cameron and directed by Cameron's wife, Kathryn Bigelow, whom he would divorce a year later. Despite their marriage ending, Cameron started working on a screenplay for Bigelow to direct titled *Strange Days*.

Strange Days is a thriller about an ex-cop and street hustler named Lenny Nero, who peddles illegal "clips" of digital recordings called "playbacks": unsavory 30-minute

The sci-fi police drama *Strange Days*, starring Ralph Fiennes and Angela Bassett, was written by Cameron and directed by Cameron's third wife Kathryn Bigelow. Unlike Cameron's other projects, the film did not perform well at the box office.

experiences of people's lives. It's a dirty business, and when someone slips Lenny a killer's clip of a brutal murder, Lenny must find the killer before he strikes again. *Strange Days* was produced by Lightstorm Entertainment and eventually released in 1995, but it was not well received by audiences or critics.

After meeting while at work on the first *Terminator* movie, Cameron and actress Linda Hamilton began a stormy romance on the set of *T2*, which soon led to marriage and later divorce.

Chapter 7

Lies and Secrets

CAMERON TENDS TO fall in love with women he works with, and Linda Hamilton was no exception. After *Terminator 2: Judgment Day*, Cameron and Hamilton moved in together; their daughter, Josephine Archer Cameron, was born in 1993. She was Cameron's first child and Hamilton's second. Shortly after Josephine's birth, Hamilton moved out. She and Cameron soon reconciled, and their stormy relationship continued on and off for the next several years.

Meanwhile, Cameron was involved in two important projects: creating his own special effects company and making another Arnold Schwarzenegger film titled *True Lies*.

In 1993, Cameron teamed up with ILM Vice President Scott Ross and Academy Award-winning special effects artist Stan Winston to create Digital Domain, a digital studio which specializes in photo-realistic animation, or computer graphic imagery (CGI). IBM and Cox Enterprises were the financial backers.

Digital Domain's first order of business was doing visual effects for *True Lies*, the first of 12 movies 20th Century Fox was paying Cameron $500 million to direct or produce over five years. The contract stipulated that Cameron would have complete creative control and that Lightstorm Entertainment would get a substanial share of any profits, provided Cameron did not exceed a studio budget of $70 million for each film. To begin work on *True Lies*, Cameron, Ross, and Winston had to move fast to locate a building, recruit personnel, and obtain the necessary equipment to launch Digital Domain.

Arnold Schwarzenegger had proposed the idea for *True Lies* over lunch with Cameron in spring of 1992 after seeing a French film called *La Totale!* In the film, a mild-mannered bureaucrat is really a daring and dashing secret agent. Of course, Schwarzenegger saw himself in the lead role.

Cameron immediately liked the idea, viewing it as a James Bond movie with the "schizophrenic nature of marriage" as a subplot. He changed the bureaucrat to a computer salesman named Harry Tasker, made him a CIA agent, and threw in a mousy wife and rebellious teenage daughter. Cameron seemed especially drawn to the concept of a CIA agent giving so much of himself on the job that there is very little left for his family at the end of the day.

In a 1994 interview with *Entertainment Weekly's* Anne Thompson, Cameron talked frankly about trying to balance work and family time in his own marriages: "[My previous wives] were both film professionals, both as workaholic as I am. If you're in a relationship with someone who understands the drive because they're driven, then you run the risk of driving in different directions. All my movies are about something I've experienced." Referring to his relationship with Hamilton, he added, "I had a daughter 16 months ago and haven't seen her nearly as much as I would have wanted. It's a big strain."

Once Cameron had developed Harry Tasker's character, Cameron went to work on Tasker's wife, Helen. Cameron wanted to create a tough, independent woman audiences would respond to, not unlike Lt. Ripley in *Aliens* and Sarah Connor in the *Terminator* films.

But when Cameron proposed Jamie Lee Curtis play Helen Tasker, Schwarzenegger reportedly protested, saying Curtis wasn't right for the role. Everyone's fears were laid to rest, however, as soon as Schwarzenegger and Curtis met.

"Arnold loves to goose people when he first meets them," Cameron recalls. "Jamie goosed right back and they were off. There's a chemistry about them together. They're both totally vulgar."

In *True Lies*, Cameron returns to a favorite theme: nuclear war. Harry Tasker must prevent Islamic terrorists from launching a nuclear attack from inside the United States. When the terrorists kidnap Tasker's daughter (Eliza Dushku), he and his wife both come to the rescue—and fall in love all over again in the process.

In the action thriller *True Lies*, Cameron paired *Terminator* star Arnold Schwarzenegger with actress Jamie Lee Curtis. Arnold had approached Cameron with the idea for the film, centering on a spy who conceals his daring work from his wife.

Cameron wanted spectacular special effects for the many action sequences in the film, so he hired John Bruno, who had won an Oscar for his work on *The Abyss*. Bruno and Cameron worked closely together to make the climactic scenes in the movie as realistic as possible. In one sequence, Tasker flies a Harrier jump jet to the top of a Miami office building to take out an entire floor of terrorists, then rescues his daughter who must fall from a construction crane onto Tasker's jet.

Rather than use traditional blue screen projection or photo-realistic animation to simulate the hero flying over downtown Miami, Cameron and Bruno decided to build a motion control apparatus on the roof of an office building 250 feet up. This machine would move a life-size model of the jet as if it were flying.

The 46-foot aircraft model weighed four tons and was attached to a 120-foot crane as well as safety wires. A propane gun, which shot flames, was installed to simulate a rapid-fire weapon. Schwarzenegger had to sit in the hot cockpit of this jet for hours, pitching and swaying to digitally-placed sound and visual effects, such as whizzing missiles, gunfire, and exhaust smoke. Cameron also paid $20,000 an hour to shoot scenes with two authentic Marine Corps Harrier jets (valued at $33 million a piece), plus four helicopters.

Another challenging scene was a land-air high speed chase on the Seven Mile Bridge connecting two Florida Keys islands. Traffic was halted for 15 minutes so Cameron could film the entire bridge; then he spent between $2 million and $3 million to blow up a one-fifth scale model of the bridge. For a scene depicting Helen's car going off the bridge, Cameron filmed an actual car falling off another bridge with a section removed for boats to go through.

In the movie, right before Helen Tasker's car goes over the bridge, she grabs a rope ladder suspended from a helicopter and is carried through the air to safety. In reality, Curtis was suspended by a 250-foot cable and *lowered* into the car from the helicopter while Cameron filmed her from inside the helicopter above. Then the film was *reversed* to create the illusion of her going *up*, when in fact she was going *down*.

The scene was a highlight for Curtis. "It was fun," she says. "Jim is the most safety-conscious person on the set."

Like *Terminator 2*, *True Lies* went over budget, so to pay his bills, Cameron renegotiated his contract with Fox Studios. The new deal was that Fox would continue to finance the film, but Cameron would only make three movies for Fox, not 12; other films would be made on a case-by-case basis. Furthermore, Fox could tap into a film's profits to recoup their investment if necessary. Most important to Cameron, however, was that he would retain creative control over his movies.

Cameron is accustomed to being criticized for over-spending. "I'm not afraid of taking risks with an awful lot of money," he told reporter Anne Thompson after *True Lies* was released in the summer of 1994. "The more successful *Terminator 2* was, the less it [actually] cost. The less successful *Last Action Hero* was, the more it cost."

Unfortunately, *True Lies* did not do that well at the box office. Its first weekend take was a respectable $25.5 million, but ticket sales went downhill from there. Although the total domestic income was eventually $149 million, the film had cost about $120 million to make. The movie was no match for summer hits like *Forrest Gump* and Disney's *The Lion King*. Although *True Lies* did win an Oscar nomination for Best Visual Effects several months later, movie critics remained unimpressed.

The film also became the center of controversy when Arab-American advocacy groups protested *True Lies* on

To create one of *True Lies*' most thrilling scenes, actress Jamie Lee Curtis was lowered by a cable from a helicopter to a car. Cameron then ran the sequence in reverse (combined with computer effects) to show Curtis being lifted from the car before it plunges from a bridge.

opening day in cities across the country, claiming Cameron portrayed Arabs as "violent, religious zealots."

Cameron's response to allegations that his film perpetuated race and gender stereotypes was blunt: "It was a very tongue-in-cheek shoot-'em-up. And you know what? I am not a p.c. [politically correct], candy-assed director."

Now that *True Lies* was finished, Cameron could pursue a project he had been secretly working on for two years. He hoped to make a film about the sinking of the *Titanic*, the worst disaster in maritime history. And he wanted the Russians to help him.

The *Titanic* left Southampton, England, April 9, 1912, bound for New York. She was 11 stories high and the length of three football fields; she boasted a full-sized gymnasium, a squash court, Turkish baths, restaurants, parlors, swimming pools, and indoor gardens. Her double-bottomed hull, divided into 16 water-tight compartments, and automatic doors for sealing flooded areas, were considered state-of-the-art disaster protection.

Nevertheless, five days after leaving England, she struck an iceberg in the North Atlantic Ocean and sank within three hours, taking 1,513 passengers with her. Only 711 passengers survived, mostly women and children who had been ordered into a small number of lifeboats. Sixty-five percent of the fatalities were poor passengers, confined to steerage compartments below and hampered by a lack of information and assistance when they tried to escape to the upper deck.

Cameron had always been fascinated by shipwrecks and had even jotted down several notes after seeing a 1987 National Geographic Explorer documentary about the ill-fated ship:

In 1912, Titanic was the most luxurious liner in the world, featuring restaurants, gymnasiums, squash courts, and indoor gardens. Although her designers boasted that she was unsinkable, an iceberg ripped through her hull and flooded many of her watertight compartments, leading to her rapid demise.

Do story with bookends of present day scene of wreck using submersibles intercut with memory of a survivor and recreated scenes of the night of the sinking. A crucible of human values under stress. A certainty of slowly impending doom (metaphor). Division of men doomed and women and children saved by custom of the times. Many dramatic moments of separation, heroism, and cowardice, civility versus animal aggression. Needs a mystery or driving plot element woven through with all this as a background.

The idea was put on hold, however, while Cameron worked on *The Abyss* and *Terminator 2*. Then in 1992 Cameron saw a CBS documentary titled *Treasures of the Deep*, which was directed and produced by Al Giddings who had spent a summer on a Russian research vessel called the *Akademik Mstislav Keldysh*. The film featured two miniature submarines capable of diving below 12,000 feet.

Cameron became excited—and determined. He wanted to charter these small submarines, so he could film the wreck of the *Titanic* for the opening sequences of the film he now intended to write, direct, and produce. But he needed Giddings' help to convince the Russians.

Giddings had been underwater photography director for *The Abyss*. He and Cameron had not parted on the best of terms, but Cameron was so excited and so insistent that a feature-length film could be made about the *Titanic* that Giddings was willing to work with Cameron again. They decided they would go to Moscow to ask for the Russians' cooperation. Cameron and Giddings named this top-secret venture "Big Boat."

The *Keldysh* and its two submersibles, *Mir 1* and *Mir 2* ("mir" meaning "peace"), were owned by the P.P. Shirshov Scientific Insitute of Oceanology. Cameron hoped to persuade Dr. Anatoly Sagalevitch, director of Shirshov's Deep Manned Submersibles Laboratory and commander in chief of the *Keldysh*, that making a Hollywood movie was a good idea. Cameron wanted access to both *Mir 1* and *Mir 2,* so that one submersible could carry a remote-controlled camera and one could be filmed exploring the *Titanic.* Paula Parisi, author of *Titanic and the Making of James Cameron*, describes the *Mirs'* state-of-the-art capabilities:

> The subs dove untethered, run by high-powered, energy-efficient French batteries that cost roughly $1 million each. The batteries drove all sub functions, including main propulsion, on dives that typically lasted 18 hours but had gone as long as 28. In a pinch they could sustain emergency life support for up to five days.

Furthermore, both *Mirs* were able to spotlight, photograph, and lift objects (using two hydraulic arms), as well as retrieve biological and geological specimens.

On board the *Keldysh,* Cameron was immediately impressed, both with the technology and the hardworking crew, with whom he developed an instant rapport. The night before Cameron and Giddings were to return to America, one of the crew threw a dinner party for them in his tiny apartment.

During dinner, Dr. Sagalevitch began a series of vodka toasts. By the time the toasts were finished, Cameron, who is not a heavy drinker, remembered feeling like he was going to die. It was worth it, however, when he heard Sagalevitch proclaim at the end of the evening: "We do it! We make Hollywood movie!"

Back in the states, Cameron stayed in touch with Sagalevitch and the Shirshov Insitute for two years, negotiating ways to use and pay for the use of the *Keldysh* and *Mir* submersibles.

When Cameron finished shooting *True Lies*, the time seemed right to make his desire known to Hollywood.

The search for the wreck of Titanic put new submersible technology to the test. Here, the research ship *Keldysh* lowers a mini-sub designed to withstand the extreme pressures of deep water. Cameron used the *Mir 1* and *2* to film the opening scenes for the film.

Parisi reports that the defining moment occurred when Cameron received a fax from Sagalevitch, which read: "There comes a time in one's life when you must do something extraordinary."

"Something extraordinary" was making *Titanic*.

Titanic was by far Cameron's most ambitious undertaking. Budget and technical problems plagued the film from the start, and forced a delay of the film's release from summer to December 1997.

Chapter 8

Iceberg Ahead!

CAMERON KNEW THAT because two other *Titanic* movies had already been made, his would have to be unique. The first *Titanic*, released in 1953, stars Barbara Stanwyck and Clifton Webb. It is a tear-jerker about an estranged couple who reconcile before the wife escapes into a lifeboat with their only son. A moment later, the son gives up his seat to a woman so he can join his father on the deck. The film won an Academy Award for Best Screenplay and Best Story.

The second film, *A Night to Remember* (British, 1958), was viewed by critics as the more historically accurate, depicting, for example, another ocean liner's failure to respond to *Titanic's* distress signals despite being only 10 miles away.

Like previous filmmakers, Cameron saw the sinking of the *Titanic* as a great story with all the right elements: compelling characters, suspense, conflict, cosmic irony, and an unbelievable climax. Cameron says:

> *Titanic* still captures our imaginations after 85 years because her story is like a great novel that really happened: the juxtaposition of rich and poor, the gender roles played out until death (women first), the stoicism and nobility of a bygone era, the magnificence of the great ship matched only in scale by the folly of the men who drove her hell-bent through the darkness. And above all the lesson: that life is uncertain, the future unknowable . . . the unthinkable possible.

But what could Cameron say that hadn't already been said in previous films? He decided he needed to tell the story against a backdrop of two characters that *contemporary* audiences would respond to—an "emotional lightning rod," as he put it.

The emotional lightning rod became a modern day Romeo and Juliet named Jack and Rose. Cameron decided to model the drifter-artist Jack Dawson after author and adventurer Jack London. Rose DeWitt Bukater would be a society woman unhappily engaged to Caledon Hockley (Billy Zane), the son of a Pittsburgh steel tycoon. When Jack and Rose fall in love, Rose's fiancé is determined to drive them apart, even as the ship fills with water and everyone scrambles to the lifeboats.

Fearing the worst, Jack tries to convince Rose to save herself by getting into a lifeboat, but she refuses. After Jack and Rose plunge into the icy water together, Jack sacrifices his life for Rose, but not before getting her to

In pitching *Titanic* to film companies, Cameron described the film as "Romeo and Juliet on a ship." The result was an Oscar-winning hit that made household names out of stars Leonardo DiCaprio and Kate Winslet.

promise him that she will go on living, no matter what.

The movie opens with Rose (Gloria Stuart), now 101, telling her story to fortune hunter Brock Lovett (Bill Paxton) who is searching *Titanic's* wreck for a lost diamond necklace once belonging to Rose. At the conclusion of Rose's story, Lovett realizes that the Titanic is much more than a shipwreck waiting to be plundered for wealth and fame: it is the story of the human spirit at its darkest but finest moment.

Despite the romantic plotline, Cameron was determined

to be as factual as possible when it came to *Titanic's* demise. As Cameron has said, "My first goal was to do a love story . . . and secondly to recreate the sinking very accurately."

After offering to give up half his salary to get Twentieth Century Fox and Paramount Pictures interested, Cameron spent six months reading American and British boards of inquiry reports, as well as the extensive research of historians Walter Lord and Don Lynch.

Cameron took detailed notes on the chronological order of events, from *Titanic's* collision with the iceberg until the ship's disappearance into the ocean, including anecdotal information about the crew and passengers in their final moments. He completed a scriptment in August 1995, then flew to Halifax, Nova Scotia, where the *Keldysh* was waiting to take him to the *Titanic* graveyard via the *Mirs* submersibles.

From the *Keldysh,* Cameron made 12 dives in 21 days. Cameron describes this experience as being similar to free-falling for hours through two-and-a-half miles of blackness in a space about the size of a clown car. Using Snoop Dog, a robotized video camera that could move about inside the wreck itself, Cameron was able to film images never seen before—even in documentaries.

"We were tremendously excited," Cameron recalls. "It was like going into King Tut's tomb . . . We found hand-carved oak paneling and columns in a remarkable state of preservation . . . I actually spent more hours observing the wreck than the passengers spent on the ship."

After Cameron returned to the States, he went to work polishing his screenplay, which he completed May 7, 1996. Next came filming the framing sequences (modern day story elements) off the shores of Halifax, Nova Scotia. There, the last night of the shoot, 80 members of the cast and crew, including Cameron, were taken to Dartmouth General

Cameron combined computerized visuals with scale models to recreate the Titanic. The largest, a 775-foot model, was nearly as impressive as the grand ship herself, and as long as a 75-story skyscraper laid on its side.

Hospital after ingesting chowder poisoned with the illegal drug PCP, or "angel dust." Although Cameron told the press he did not think the poisoning was a malicious attempt to hurt himself or the project, his staff suspected a crew member who had been recently terminated for selling drugs.

When filming was finished in Halifax, Cameron flew to Rosarito Beach, Mexico, to shoot the 1912 sequences. Here, Cameron worked in the largest and most expensive movie studio complex and outdoor filming tank in the world.

Cameron had spent $57 million to build, among other things, a nine-tenths scale model of the Titanic based on original blueprints. When completed, the 775-foot model was equivalent to a 75-story skyscraper on its side.

The outdoor filming tank, where the *Titanic* model was "launched," held 17 million gallons of seawater. An interior tank, which was used to flood sections of the ship, held five million gallons of water. Five sound stages housed elaborate sets featuring an authentically recreated five-story grand staircase and first class dining room, complete with furniture, china, glassware, and "*Titanic*" engraved silverware. Each set had to be built on big steel structures which could be plunged up and down into seawater with the help of hidden hydrolic lifts. "We had to create all this opulence," Cameron jokes, "and then sink it!"

Sinking the *Titanic* and filming this operation was problematic, dangerous, and expensive. But Cameron was determined to do what previous filmmakers had *not* done; that is, show the *Titanic* going down in *two* sections, not one. Early researchers had speculated that when the *Titanic* scraped the iceberg on her starboard side, water began pouring in through a 12-foot gash at about eight tons per second, quickly filling the forward watertight holds.

But after the wreck was discovered in 1985, scientists determined that the iceberg had, in fact, punctured several small holes in the first six compartments of the hull. A series of explosions in the engine room followed. By the time the last lifeboat rowed away, the flooded bow (front of the ship) had begun to sink, causing the stern (rear) to rise out of the water. As the stern reached a near vertical position, the ship broke apart and the stern dropped back down like an elevator. The bow sank first; then the stern rose again, bobbed like a cork for about five minutes, and sank rapidly. At this point, hundreds of people, hanging onto the stern, either fell or dove off to take their chances in the icy water; most died of hypothermia within minutes.

Cameron wanted his epic film to set the record straight, which meant he had to figure out a way to tilt the poop deck of a 90-foot stern and then show passengers falling off of it. Cameron decided about 150 extras would be tied to the sides of the deck and about 100 stunt performers would roll down the middle, slamming into metal objects that were actually made of foam. The stern would be tilted just 30 degrees. Trick photography would make the stern seem higher.

Unfortunately, even at 30 degrees, the stuntmen slid quickly down the stern, often bumping into each other; when minor injuries resulted, Cameron decided to abandon live actors in favor of "synthespians," realistic digital humans who appear to fall or fly off the stern as it sinks. During production, Cameron's motto was "We either do it right or do it till we get it right." So it wasn't unusual for Cameron to shoot a scene 10 or 12 times before he was satisfied.

Cameron had high expectations of his crew as well. Assistant Director Kristie Sills says Cameron's perfectionism always intimidates his crew at first. "He can do everyone's job, usually better than they can," she explains. "So when he sees incompetence or weakness or insecurity, it frustrates him, and he'll step in and take over."

For the scene following the *Titanic*'s collision with the iceberg, Cameron wanted real chunks of ice sliding across the deck. Production consultant Marty Katz remembers Cameron impatiently taking an ax away from a crew member who was hacking away at a hundred pound block of ice too slowly. In demonstrating to his crew how he wanted the ice chopped, Cameron, says Katz, set "an unbelievable standard" that earned him a reputation for being downright crazy. But Cameron admirers say this behavior simply exemplifies Cameron's conviction to never ask his cast and crew to do something he would not do himself.

James Muro, a steadicam operator, remembers filming one last scene before the crew was to begin a two-week vacation. At the end of an 18-hour day, Muro and other camera operators had to shoot a huge implosion of water through a glass door. Cameron took extra precautions and shot one of the more treacherous underwater scenes himself.

Another difficult shot occurred when Cameron positioned nine cameras to film hundreds of gallons of water pouring in through a ceiling on the ship. Cameron, as well as other crew members, wore a wetsuit and scuba diving apparatus while holding onto his camera "for dear life."

However, just like the protagonist Cameron had created for *True Lies,* Cameron found himself once again trying to juggle his professional and personal commitments. In July 1997, he took one of only two days off during a 160-day shoot to marry his girlfriend of several years, Linda Hamilton. They did not take a honeymoon.

Throughout *Titanic's* production, Cameron, ever the perfectionist, continued to edit the script, a process that would continue into postproduction and even after audience reactions in test screenings.

Cameron likens editing to sculpting. "You're taking away material to create a final form," he says. "Don't mourn the chips of marble on the floor. Don't mourn the sculpture that could have been. Celebrate what is there."

One of the scenes Cameron shortened was the one depicting Brock Lovett's exploration of the wreck; Cameron feared the scene was too much like a documentary and would bore the audience. So he retained only those images

Outside the film's romantic plot, Cameron was committed to being as historically accurate as possible in creating *Titanic*. He consulted historians and reviewed countless reports from the wreck to ensure that the film followed the facts of the sinking.

that would emphasize the human connection to the *Titanic:* a chair, a table, a photograph, reading glasses, and a doll's head.

Cameron's perfectionism and obsession with historical accuracy, no matter what the cost, led one studio executive to declare Cameron "uncontrollable."

Studios had budgeted $115 million going into the project, plus the cost of the studio facility in Mexico. However, not long into production, hidden costs began to mount on a daily basis. Sometimes, according to Cameron, the cost would jump $20 million almost overnight, mostly because no one had ever attempted to build a full-size ocean liner and then sink it. Heavy equipment alone, such as cranes, generators, and forklifts, cost a million dollars a month to rent.

Special effects were also expensive. Some shots cost as much as $400,000 because of the technology involved. Cameron had his key actors' images scanned into a computer, so their likenesses could be added digitally to scenes depicting the entire ship, such as when Jack declares, "I'm king of the world!" while standing on the bow. Other special effects helped create the illusion of *Titanic* passengers freezing in Mexico's warm waters; as actors pretended to shiver and breathe heavily, Cameron had their breath "painted" in digitally.

Cameron's "$1 million chick flick" was quickly turning into a $2 million chick flick. Embarrassed, Cameron told studio executives to take the rest of his salary. "I had not gotten them into this situation intentionally," he explains. "I was willing to take responsibility for it."

When the budget continued to career out of control, Cameron offered the studio his points (his share of any profits). It was speculated that Cameron's points and the $8 million salary he had sacrificed could total as much as $50 million if the film did better than *True Lies* or *Terminator 2*. The prospect of losing so much money did not deter Cameron, who said he preferred to lose money rather than spend three years of his life making a "bad movie."

Nevertheless, as *Titanic* neared its release date of December 19, 1997, the press repeatedly emphasized

Cameron's excessive spending, so much so that Jon Landau, one of *Titanic's* producers, came to Cameron's defense:

> *Titanic* was not an out-of-control production. It's just that everything we did cost five times more than we expected. At the time we shot the first flooding sequence in the first-class dining room, we had just put in a filtration system that would take ocean water, heat it up, and pump it into the set. That night it rained four inches. [The mud] ran into the ocean and right into our filtration system. We had people in the ocean cleaning mud, by hand, from the filters.

Cameron also bristled when he was accused of spending too much money. "Everyone acts like it's a new thing because the numbers are unprecedented," he told a reporter. "But the cost of bread is unprecedented. People make a big deal out of the fact that the real *Titanic* cost just $7 million in 1911. But today it would cost half a billion."

By the time *Titanic* opened six months behind schedule, it was the most expensive movie ever made. Including marketing and distribution costs, *Titanic* cost about $400 million.

But Cameron's persistence paid off. *Titanic* broke box office records in over 50 countries and was number one in American theaters 14 consecutive weeks, grossing $200 million in just 26 days. When *Titanic* grossed $500 million, the studios disregarded Cameron's offer to forego his points and awarded him a bonus of an undisclosed amount close to $100 million. Eventually, the film earned $1.7 billion.

Movie audiences, especially teenage girls, loved *Titanic*. Some critics were also impressed. Steve Tilley wrote that *Titanic* was sure to please everyone because it was three films in one: "a historical docudrama; a weepy love story; and a special effects bonanza."

Brian D. Johnson wrote: " . . . the ship is the film's undisputed star. From the gleaming decks to the satanic mills of the engine room, it is so massively convincing that once the iceberg rips into the hull, the historic weight of the Titanic tragedy begins to lend the narrative an irresistible momentum."

Other critics were less than complimentary, particularly with respect to the screenplay, calling the plot and dialog "corny" and "Disney-like." Some challenged the historical accuracy that Cameron had worked so hard to convey. Joseph Roquemore, author of *History Goes to the Movies,* criticized Cameron's portrayal of *Titanic's* Captain Smith as being indecisive and useless throughout the disaster, saying this portrayal "contradicts every eyewitness account of his behavior during the 160-minute interval between collision and submersion." Roquemore concluded his analysis with the comment, "Great pyrotechnics— mediocre history." Even comedian Jerry Seinfeld poked fun at *Titanic's* success in his sitcom: "What's the deal with this *Titanic* movie? You know how it ends. The ship sinks. Why not stay home and rent a video?"

Cameron felt the negative reviews of *Titanic* were unjustified, especially when he and *Titanic* began to win awards. Both the Broadcast Film Critics Association and Directors Guild of America named Cameron Best Director; he also won two Golden Globe Awards for Best Director and Best Picture as well as the MTV Movie Award for Best Picture. Most important, on Oscar night, *Titanic* won 11 Academy Awards, including Best Film Editing, Best Director, and Best Picture.

Yet, according to the press, Oscar night was a disappointment to Linda Hamilton, who was reportedly yanked by the

Titanic appealed to audiences on many levels: as historical docudrama, as a love story, and as an effects-driven disaster film. Whatever the reason, audiences kept coming back to see the film a second or third time.

arm and reprimanded by Cameron in public just hours before he took the stage to accept his awards. When questioned later if receiving 11 Oscars had changed her husband in any way, Hamilton replied, "He was always a jerk, so there's no way to really measure." She went on to say she hoped Oscar night would be the "last hurrah for *Titanic.*"

Six weeks later, Cameron moved out of their Malibu, California, home amid rumors he was having an affair with Suzy Amis, the actress who plays the granddaughter of the 101-year-old Rose in *Titanic.* According to film critic Christopher Heard, Cameron had been "drooling" over Amis on the set and "had a crush on her."

Hamilton told reporters that even though Cameron had

Cameron and wife Linda Hamilton arrive at the Golden Laurel Awards, where Cameron was nominated for the Darryl F. Zanuck Theatrical Motion Picture Producer of the Year Award for *Titanic*.

been very difficult to live with and that they had nothing in common but their daughter Josephine (now 6), their separation was quite painful. To emphasize how stressful married life with Cameron was, Hamilton commented that even on Oscar night her husband was an "absolutely miserable, miserable unhappy man."

A year after *Titanic* was released, Hamilton and Cameron divorced. Cameron and Suzie Amis were married June 4, 2000 and had a daughter named Carol on April 4, 2001. Amis is Cameron's fifth wife.

Cameron has said he does not worry about his personal image undermining his professional image. "Filmmakers are remembered for their films," he explains. "The private stuff is ultimately irrelevant. It's what made it up on the screen. And so I feel pretty good about what's made it up on the screen."

Cameron feels especially good about *Titanic's* success and still talks of his achievement with pride: "Making *Titanic* was unexplored territory. We tried a magic spell that had never been tried before and it worked."

The magic spell continues. Today, tourists pay almost $70,000 to follow in Cameron's footsteps by boarding the *Mir 1* or *Mir 2* submersible to see the *Titanic's* graveyard for themselves. Sitting two to a sub, passengers can explore the wreck for three to five hours and leave with still photographs and a video recording of what they saw, as well as their reactions.

Cameron had successfully cleared his own iceberg and was steaming ahead at full speed.

After Titanic, Cameron turned his attention to television, creating the sci-fi miniseries *Dark Angel*, starring Jessica Alba.

Chapter 9

Dark Angel

AFTER *TITANIC*, HOLLYWOOD realized that James Cameron could write, produce, and direct films in other genres besides sci-fi and horror. He was on top of his game and, most likely, could have had any project he desired. But, as Cameron has said, "with a great deal of choices comes indecision."

Initially, he hoped to direct a movie about Spiderman, his favorite comic book character who is a journalist by day and a web-spinning action hero by night. Cameron had written a script and proposed the project to Carolco Pictures in 1991 after making *Terminator 2: Judgment Day*. Unfortunately, a legal battle between several studios ensued over screen rights to the *Spiderman* series, owned by Marvel Comics. By the time the smoke cleared many years later, Cameron was committed to other projects. (Columbia Pictures' *Spider-Man* is scheduled to appear in theaters May 3, 2002.) Another proposal that interested Cameron was writing and producing a remake of *Planet of the Apes* (1968). But Cameron bailed out when he and 20th Century Fox could not agree on who would direct the film.

Cameron also flirted with the possibility of directing a futuristic virtual reality thriller he wrote titled *Avatar*. In the film, he envisioned a completely digitalized cast, as opposed to live actors. Cameron had used digital actors, or "synthespians," in *Titanic,* but they did not act or have speaking roles. They were merely computer-generated stand-ins and stunt persons. In *Avatar,* Cameron hoped to create cybernetic actors so life-like that moviegoers would not be able to tell the difference between them and live actors—even when speaking. The project, spearheaded by Digital Domain and estimated to cost at least $300 million, never came to fruition.

Then in March 1999, Cameron surprised Hollywood by suddenly turning to television as the next medium for his "narrative drive." He became partners with Charles "Chic" Eglee to create a company which produces shows exclusively for television.

"I like challenges," Cameron told reporters after announcing his decision. "After years of painting on the feature-film canvas, I'm excited to turn my creative focus to a medium that emphasizes writing, not visual spectacle. Ultimately, telling stories is what I love to do most." Cameron said the potential for telling a character's story over months or years, instead of two hours, was also appealing.

Cameron and Eglee's first order of business was to create a television sci-fi miniseries called *Dark Angel* for Fox Broadcasting. In co-writing the pilot episode for *Dark Angel*, Cameron incorporated two of his favorite elements: the strong heroine and a futuristic world in chaos.

Max, played by Jessica Alba, is a "transgenic," an adolescent female with genetically-engineered superpowers living in the year 2020. While searching for others like herself, she begins a relationship with Logan Cale (Michael Weatherly), a journalist attempting to expose and destroy the government masterminds who created Max and now want to control her.

An advanced screening of the pilot episode, which aired in October 2000, prompted this response from a television critic:

> *Dark Angel* isn't exactly warm and cuddly. It's set in an impoverished, nasty, garbage-strewn, tyrannical future, focusing on a sprightly nymphet who talks hip-hop and has moves like an outtake from *The Matrix*.

Time Magazine wrote: "We have seen the woman of the future and she kicks butt."

Nielson ratings for the pilot were very promising. A record-breaking 17.3 million viewers tuned in to *Dark Angel* instead of watching the first presidential debate between George W. Bush and Al Gore on other stations.

With *Dark Angel* underway and scoring decent reviews, Cameron turned the day-to-day operations of running the series over to Eglee, believing, "the way to keep a show alive is to create a strong team and empower them."

Meanwhile, Cameron busied himself with other projects, such as co-writing and planning to direct a sequel to *True Lies* (1994), again starring Arnold Schwarzenegger and Jamie Lee Curtis. A work in progress, *True Lies 2* has been

Combining a darkly futuristic world with a strong female character, *Dark Angel* has earned itself a large number of loyal viewers.

scheduled for production in late 2002 or early 2003 after Schwarzenegger finishes filming *Terminator 3,* which Cameron declined an invitation to write and direct.

But the project that had everyone talking was Cameron's alleged plan to convince the Russians to let him ride one of their rockets into space, much like when he had talked them into letting him use one of their submersibles to film the *Titanic* at the bottom of the North Atlantic Ocean. Rumors of Cameron's desire to travel into space started circulating when the *New York Post* reported Cameron's interest in shooting a television miniseries and IMAX film about Mars with the help of the Russian space program. There were even reports that Cameron had flown in a Russian jet to gather data on zero gravity.

Lightstorm Entertainment's president, Rae Sanchini, denied the rumors, saying Cameron was in touch with Russia merely to research the cosmonaut experience. But a Russian news agency said Cameron was indeed requesting a trip to the International Space Station (ISS) and had already undergone a medical screening and checkup at the Moscow Medico-Biological Institute the previous year.

Then in April 2001, *USA Today* reported Cameron was close to signing a contract with the Russian Aerospace Agency that would enable him to become the second civilian to take advantage of Russia's lucrative space tourism program. Cameron's permission to go was contingent on the success of California investment banker Dennis Tito's voyage into space April 28. Tito was the first to pay Russia's space program about $20 million for the privilege of visiting the ISS, against the wishes of NASA.

It was speculated that Cameron hoped to go into space in late 2002 to shoot a documentary for Fox Broadcasting, a 3-D film about outer space, and a feature-length film about a mission to Mars. Cameron also wanted to be the first civilian to walk in space.

In the *USA Today* article, NASA director Daniel Goldin said that he, too, had been approached by Cameron, but had told Cameron that criteria for implementing a civilian space program had not yet been created. Goldin said Cameron agreed to be patient and to wait for the Americans to take him into space. Goldin later told members of a U.S.

"Space tourist" Dennis Tito paid the Russian Aerospace Agency nearly 20 million dollars to visit the International Space Station. Cameron hopes to follow in Tito's footsteps but will need 18 months of training before he can lift-off.

House of Representatives panel on space and aeronautics that Cameron was "an American patriot who understood how to do this [unlike Dennis Tito]."

If Cameron is allowed to go into space, either with the Americans or Russians, he will have to undergo 18 months of intensive training beforehand.

Meanwhile, *Dark Angel* had begun its second season in fall 2001. Jessica Alba received a Golden Globe nomination for best actress in a television series, and six months after the show debuted, she and Weatherly announced their engagement in real life, which, television critics have said, is likely to result in higher ratings as more viewers tune in to watch Max and Cale's romance intensify in future episodes.

To ensure *Dark Angel* stayed viable for a second season, Cameron sat down with his creative team to brainstorm additional characters and plot lines. One idea was to develop other genetically altered humans that become a "persecuted minority"; another was to create more obstacles for Max and Cale to overcome. "I think we've come up with one that's a corker," Cameron told the *Akron Beacon Journal* in July 2001.

After helping to generate ideas for future *Dark Angel* episodes, Cameron embarked on another project in August: returning to the *Keldysh* to film scenes of the *Titanic's* wreck for a 3-D IMAX-style documentary titled *Ghosts of the Abyss*. Cameron's remote-controlled video cameras explored other parts of the ship that had not been visible since 1912. Cameron also shot footage of the sunken German World War II battleship, the *Bismark*.

Ghosts of the Abyss was scheduled for release late in 2002, but through September 2001, *Titanic* fans were invited to witness live broadcasts of the expedition on Earthship.TV, an interactive entertainment website created by John David Cameron (James Cameron's younger brother) and John Skeel. Reruns of the edited footage and comments by the cast and crew are still available for viewing on the site.

Also in the fall of 2001, Lightstorm Entertainment announced the development and production of a live-action version of the Top Cow comic book, *Fathom,* featuring the adventures of a female Olympic swimmer and marine biologist with mysterious powers. Cameron has not yet decided whether he will direct the film, but if he does, movie fans will certainly pay eight dollars to see it.

James Cameron is one of the most accomplished and controversial filmmakers of the twentieth century. For *Titanic* alone, his awards include two Golden Globes, three Academy Awards, the 1999 People's Choice Award, and the American Cinema Editors' 1999 Filmmaker of the Year Award. He is also the recipient of honorary degrees from three Canadian universities, including Brock, Carleton, and Ryerson Polytechnic.

Four years after making *Titanic,* Cameron remains one of the world's highest paid entertainers and is considered the second most bankable director in the film industry after Steven Spielberg. He has been called "extraordinary," "brilliant," "relentless," and "a control freak." So it's no surprise that Cameron keeps two handwritten Post-It notes taped to his computer monitor. They read: "break new ground" and "good enough isn't."

Cameron says these statements reflect the way he lives and works as a writer, director, and producer. But he insists that he is not driven to create enjoyable and memorable films because of his quest for perfection or an inflated ego.

Says Cameron, "It's not about perfectionism . . . It's more of a question of striving for excellence . . . It's not about my ego. It's about the film taking on a life of its own, having its *own* ego. And we all serve that. We serve that life."

Cameron tells aspiring film directors to find the path that's right for them, based on their talents, strengths, and weaknesses, and to never take "no" for an answer.

One of the most admired and celebrated directors in film, Cameron's commitment and perfectionism have earned him a place as one of the world's highest-paid entertainers, with fans eagerly awaiting his next project.

"Success in Hollywood is not measured on talent alone," Cameron advises. "Persistence and determination are the keys to success; then comes talent."

Certainly, the truck driver from Chippewa who became an Oscar-winning director knows what he's talking about.

1954 James Cameron is born in Kapuskasing, Canada; family moves to Chippewa, a suburb of Niagara Falls, Canada

1971 Cameron graduates from Stamford Collegiate High School; family moves to Orange County, California; briefly attends California State University at Fullerton

1974 Cameron marries Sharon Williams, a waitress who will later be the inspiration for Sarah Connor in *Terminator* and *Terminator 2: Judgment Day*

1978 Cameron co-writes and directs *Xenogenesis*, a 10-minute science fiction film

1979 Cameron begins work as a miniature model builder at Roger Corman's New World Pictures

1980 Cameron becomes art director for Corman's *Battle Beyond the Stars*

1981 Cameron becomes special effects director of photography for Corman's *Escape from New York*; also works as a production designer and second unit director for *Galaxy of Terror*; leaves New World Pictures to direct his first feature-length film, *Piranha 2: The Spawning*

1982 Serves as a design consultant for *Android*; divorces Sharon Williams; begins writing *The Terminator* with producer Gale Anne Hurd, which Hemdale Pictures allows Cameron to direct; Cameron also co-writes the screenplay for *Rambo: First Blood Part II* and begins writing the screenplay for *Aliens,* which he will also direct

1984 *Terminator* released

1985 *Rambo: First Blood Part II* is released; Cameron marries Gale Anne Hurd.

1986 *Aliens* is released and wins Academy Awards for Best Visual Effects and Best Sound Effects Editing; Cameron gets studio approval to write and direct *The Abyss*

1989 *The Abyss* is released; wins an Academy Award for Best Visual Effects; Cameron divorces Gale Anne Hurd and marries action movie director Kathryn Bigelow

1990 Cameron creates Lightstorm Entertainment, which will produce *Terminator 2: Judgment Day*

1991 Cameron produces Bigelow's *Point Break*; he also writes, directs, and produces *Terminator 2: Judgment Day,* which wins four Academy Awards for Best Makeup, Best Sound, Best Sound Effects Editing, and Best Visual Effects; *Terminator 2* also wins the MTV Movie Award and People's Choice Award for Best Film

1992 Cameron divorces Bigelow and begins a relationship with *Terminator* actress Linda Hamilton

1993 Josephine Archer Cameron is born to Hamilton and Cameron; Cameron creates special effects company, Digital Domain, which will handle the special effects for future Cameron movies, beginning with *True Lies.*

1994 *True Lies* is released; Cameron completes screenplay for and plans to produce *Strange Days*, directed by Bigelow

1995 *Strange Days* is released; Cameron finishes screenplay for *Titanic* and begins shooting

1997 *Titanic* is released

1998 *Titanic* wins 11 Academy Awards, including Best Picture, Best Director, and Best Editing for Cameron; Cameron also wins two Golden Globe Awards for Best Director and Best Picture as well the Best Director Award from the Directors Guild of America; receives honorary degrees from three Canadian universities; divorces Linda Hamilton to begin a relationship with Suzy Amis, an actress who plays Rose's granddaughter in *Titanic*

1999 Cameron continues to win awards for *Titanic*, including the People's Choice Award for Favorite Dramatic Motion Picture and the Golden Eddie Award for Filmmaker of the Year

2000 Cameron marries Suzy Amis and creates *Dark Angel* television series for Fox Broadcasting

2001 Carol Cameron is born to Cameron and Amis; Cameron begins work on *True Lies 2* and a documentary titled *Ghosts of the Abyss*

1978 *Xenogenesis*
Writer (with William Wisher)
Director

1980 *Battle Beyond the Stars*
Art Director

1981 *Escape from New York*
Matte Artwork/Special Effects Director of Photography

Galaxy of Terror
Production Designer
Unit Director

Piranha 2: The Spawning
Director

1982 *Android*
Design Consultant

1984 *The Terminator*
Writer (with Gale Anne Hurd)
Director

1985 *Rambo: First Blood Part II*
Writer (with Sylvester Stallone)

1986 *Aliens*
Writer (with Walter Hill and David Giler)
Director

1989 *The Abyss*
Writer
Director

1991 *Point Break*
Executive Producer

Terminator 2: Judgment Day
Writer (with William Wisher)
Director
Producer

1994 *True Lies*
Writer
Director
Producer

1995   *Strange Days*
Writer (with Jay Cocks)
Producer (with Steven Charles Jaffe)

1996   *Terminator 2: 3-D [Battle Across Time]*
Writer
Director

1997   *Titanic*
Writer
Director
Producer (with Jon Landau)

2000-2002   *Dark Angel* (Television series)
Writer (pilot episode)
Executive Producer

2002   *Ghosts of the Abyss* (Documentary)
Director

2003-2004   *True Lies 2* (pending)
Writer (with Jeff Easton)
Director
Producer

Ansen, David, et al. "Our Titanic Love Affair." *Newsweek,*
23 Feb. 1998: 58.

"As Seen in...Cruise Special." *The Australian,* 28 April 2001.

Barnard, Elissa. "It's Full Steam Ahead for Unsinkable Cameron."
Halifax Chronicle-Herald, 26 Nov. 1997.

Bart, Peter. "The King of the TV World." *Variety,* 2 Oct. 2000: 4.

Brouwer, Alexandra, and Thomas Lee Wright. *Working in Hollywood.*
New York: Crown Publishers, Inc., 1990.

Cameron, James. Foreword. *James Cameron's Titanic.* By Edward W.
Marsh. New York: HarperPerennial, 1997.

———. Introduction. *Strange Days.* New York: Penguin Books, 1995.

———. Introduction/Foreword. *Terminator 2: Judgment Day.* By James
Cameron and William Wisher. New York: Applause Books, 1991.

"Cameron Dives into Fathom." *Mr.Showbiz,* 5 Sept. 2001. Movies.com.

"Cameron Not King of Planet." *Mr.Showbiz,* 25 March 1999.
Movies.com.

"Chippewa." *Chippewa/Ojibway/Anishinabe Literature,*
15 Oct. 2001. Indians.org.

Cook, David A. *A History of Narrative Film.* 3rd ed. New York:
W.W. Norton & Co., 1996.

Craig, Jeff. "Making Waves: James Cameron's Computer-Generated
'Synthespians' Have Some Actors Nervous." *Express,*
28 March 1998.

Day, Patrick. "20,000 Stories Under the Sea." *Los Angeles Times,*
13 Nov. 2001.

Ebert, Roger. "Review of Aliens." *Chicago Sun Times,* 18 July 1986.

Emery, Robert J. *The Director: Take Two.* New York:
TV Books, 2000.

Encore Presentation of *The Directors: Films of James Cameron.*
Produced by Robert J. Emery and American Film Institute for
Media Entertainment, Inc. 2000.

Factor, Sue. "People's Choice Winners." *USA Today,* 12 Jan. 1999: 2D.

"The Facts: James Cameron." *E!Online,* 4 Oct. 2001. Eonline.com

Field, Syd. *Four Screenplays* (1994) *Joshua's James Cameron Web Site – Biography,* 9 Sept. 2001. Sweetbomb.com.

Frakes, Randall. *Titanic: James Cameron's Illustrated Screenplay.* New York: A Harper Entertainment Book, 1998.

France-Nuriddin, Roxie, ed. *100 Years of Hollywood.* Alexandria, VA: Time Life Books, 1999.

Glennon, Lorraine, ed. *The 20th Century: An Illustrated History of our Lives and Times.* North Dighton, MA: JG Press, Inc., 2000.

Goodale, Gloria. "Director's Answer to 'Xena,' 'Buffy.'" *Christian Science Monitor,* 25 Aug. 2000:19.

"Hamilton on Cameron." *Mr. Showbiz,* 22 Jan. 1999. Movies.com.

Heard, Christopher. *Dreaming Aloud: The Life and Films of James Cameron.* Toronto: Doubleday Canada Limited,1998.

Heldenfels, R.D. "Producer Tells of New Plans for 'Dark Angel.'" *Acron Beacon Journal,* 20 July 2001.

Hobson, Louis. "Full Steam Ahead." *Calgary Sun,* 29 March 1998.

——. "Sail of the Century: Blockbuster Steams from Port Friday." *Express*, 14 Dec. 1997.

——. "This Titanic No Disaster." *Sun Entertainment,* 13 Jan. 1998.

——. "Titanic Refund." *Calgary Sun,* 26 Jan. 1998.

"Hollywood Director Negotiating Flight to ISS with Russia." *ITAR-TASS*, 28 April 2001.

"James Cameron Biography." *Filmmakers Magazine,* 4 Oct. 2001. Filmmakers.com.

"James Cameron: King of the Idiot Box." *Mr. Showbiz,* 10 Sept. 1998. Movies.com.

Johnson, Brian D. "Titanic Ambition." *Maclean's,* 8 Dec. 1997:86.

"Journey to Mars." *Upcoming Movies,* 5 Oct. 2000. Upcomingmovies.com.

Kael, Pauline. *State of the Art.* New York: E.P. Dutton, 1985.

Karp, Alan. "Terminator Review." *Box Office Magazine,* Jan. 1985. Boxofficemagazine.com.

Kirkland, Bruce. "The Abyss out on DVD." *Toronto Sun,* 27 March 2000.

Knolle, Sharon. "King of Outer Space?" *Mr. Showbiz,* 3 Oct. 2000. ABCNEWS.com.

Kydd, Paul. "User Comments: Xenogenesis (1978)." *Xenogenesis,* 3 Jan. 2001. Imdb.com.

Landau, Jon. "Water—Everywhere." *Newsweek,* 28 June 1999:78.

Lodge, Jack, et al. *1930-1990 Hollywood: Sixty Great Years.* New York: Barnes & Noble, Inc. 1996.

"Man Overboard." *People,* 11 May 1998:64.

McHugh, Kenna. *Breaking into Film.* Princeton: Peterson's, 1999.

Millar, Dan. *Special Effects.* Secaucus, NJ: Chartwell Books, 1990.

"The Name Game." *Variety,* 17 July 2000:5.

"New Baby, NASA Praise for Cameron." *Mr. Showbiz,* 2 May 2001. Movies.com.

Parisi, Paula. *Titanic and the Making of James Cameron.* New York: Newmarket Press, 1998.

"People in the News." *FOF News Digest,* 31 Dec. 1994. Facts.com.

Poniewozik, James. "2020 Vision." *Time,* 2 Oct. 2000:86.

Rap, Curtis. *James Cameron Biography.* 2 Nov. 2001. http://www.geocities.com/Hollywood/picture/1736/bio.htm

Roquemore, Joseph. *History Goes to the Movies.* New York: Doubleday, 1999.

Skal, David J. *The Monster Show: A Cultural History of Horror.* New York: W.W. Norton & Co., 1993.

"Special Effects: Titanic and Beyond." *Nova Online* (Nova Scientific Institute), Nov. 2000.

"Spending Time Wisely." *Maclean's,* 12 June 1995:54.

"Spielberg is Bankable." *Newsmakers*, 17 Nov. 2000. Asian Age Online.

Spelling, Ian. "Director Under Pressure." *Starlog Magazine,* Jan. 1990.

Stoynoff, Natasha. "Floating Dreams." *Toronto Sun,* 14 Dec. 1997.

———. "That Sinking Feeling." *Toronto Sun,* 3 May 1998.

Swanson, Tim. "'Titanic' Titan Having a Blast." *Variety,* 30 April 2001:4.

Thompson, Anne. "Five True Lies About James Cameron." *Entertainment Weekly,* 29 July 1994.

Tilley, Steve. "Let's Sink Titanic Hype." *Express,* 28 Feb. 1998.

"Titanic Director Tipped as Next Space Tourist." *The Australian,* 30 April 2001.

"True Lies 2." *Upcoming Movies,* 27 Aug. 2001. Upcomingmovies.com.

Tyrangiel, Josh. "People." *Time Canada,* 21 May 2001:64.

Picture Credits

About the author

Bonnie McMeans is a professor of English at Delaware County Community College and a freelance writer whose work has appeared in *Cobblestone* and *Appleseeds.* She has a master's degree in journalism and a bachelor's degree in social anthropology. She lives with her husband and three children in Havertown, Pennsylvania. This is her first book.